The
Citizen
Investor

by
Phil Dow

Library of Congress Cataloging-in-Publication Data

Dow, Phil S.   Brown, Paul B.

The citizen investor: the power of ownership/by Phil Dow with Paul B. Brown

1st edition

Includes bibliographical references.

ISBN 0-9743190-0-7

1. Investments.   2. Finance, personal.   I. Title.

RBC DAIN – A division of Royal Bank of Canada

Developed by Bright House & Book Productions, LLC for RBC Dain

Typeset in Adobe Garamond font.

ISBN 0-9743190-0-7

EAN – 9780974319001

This publication is designed to provide accurate and authoritative information in
regard to the subject matter covered. It is sold with the understanding that neither the
author(s) nor the publisher is engaged in rendering legal, accounting or other professional
service. If legal advice or other expert assistance is required, the services of a competent
professional person should be sought.

> *— From a Declaration of Principles jointly adopted by a Committee*
> *of the American Bar Association and a Committee of Publishers.*

Copies of THE CITIZEN INVESTOR are available at special quantity discount for sales
promotions or for use in corporate training programs. For more information, please write
to the Director of Public Relations, RBC DAIN, Sixty South Sixth Street, Minneapolis,
MN 55402. Or contact Client Distribution Services at (212) 223-2969.

10 9 8 7 6 5 4 3 2

To the financial consultants I have worked with and served over the last 32 years. I have enjoyed the unique privilege of working with some of the finest professionals in this industry. It is to this hardworking group of men and women and the clients they serve that I dedicate this book.

ACKNOWLEDGEMENTS

Three years is an eternity in today's business world. That's how long it took to create this book. During that time there were many moments, particularly during the dark days following 9/11, when I was convinced it would never be published. But, like so many things in my life, the ups and downs happened for a reason and I am convinced that *The Citizen Investor* is finally being published at the right time, a time when individuals are beginning to recognize that, as it always does, the market recovers.

I would like to thank the people who directly made it happen: writer Paul Brown, agent/quarterback John Larson, and the PR professionals, Dan Callahan and Kevin Cockett. RBC Dain management has been incredibly supportive and encouraging. Thanks to Irv Weiser, Ron Tschetter, Charley Grose, Dick McFarland, Peter Armenio, and Brian Peters.

Thanks to my colleagues on the Private Client Research team. Their support and collective professionalism has enhanced my job, helped me grow, and provided to clients the advantage of an independent research perspective.

Many people helped me understand and develop the precepts that make up this book. Above all of them, I will always remember the counsel and example of professionalism set by Dick Kimball at Kidder Peabody.

Personally, I am fortunate to be the living legacy of my parents who, in their caring way, taught me what matters in life. Also, my gratitude to Bill W.

And, thanks to all the individual investors who have heard my ideas over the past 17 years. In cities across the country, I have met and talked to thousands of citizen investors. Thanks to them for listening to me and believing in the great American experiment that has created more wealth, more democratically, than any other economic system at any time in history.

TABLE OF CONTENTS

"Bear markets are those periods when stocks return to their rightful owners." –Unknown

Warning:
The book you have chosen to read does not follow the conventional wisdom.

The conventional wisdom of the early 21st century says that this is the wrong time to be writing a book about investing for the long term. Everywhere we seem to turn, there is another piece of earth-shattering news that is driving markets down: war, recession, scandal, and terror in the streets. About the only thing we've missed has been a plague of locusts in Central Park.

Of course, the conventional wisdom is based in reality—they don't call it wisdom without reason. All this bad news is real; there is a lot to worry about in the world. But just as we were irrationally exuberant as stocks went up, we are equally irrationally negative when they have inevitably come down. Despite the equally real positives out there—the remarkable productivity gains we have made, the historically low interest rates, the lack of inflation, and the power technology offers for improving our everyday lives—we can't seem to focus on anything but the daily horror stories. Our emotions are running away with our intellect.

I think the conventional wisdom is wrong. I believe this is the precise moment to turn our sights to a longer-term strategy, one that depends on wealth creation through ownership, the confidence created by owning dominant companies, and the incredible power of time.

These concepts form the basis of *The Citizen Investor*, an approach to living and investing that relies on hope, confidence, and a straightforward understanding of risk.

Even if you don't buy my long-term positive assumption and aside from when you believe the market will recover— today, tomorrow, or in ten years—there is one overwhelming reason to consider becoming a Citizen Investor, even in the midst of bad times: the reality of what saving for retirement will mean in the 21st century. By living longer as a nation, we are requiring more capital than ever, while, at the same time, the companies we work for have put each of us in charge of our own retirement packages. This combination leaves most people with the need to plan their own retirements, but no one has given them the means or the knowledge of how to do it. In effect, we are an army of investors who have never been trained for combat.

INTRODUCTION

That training requires a discipline of stock ownership, not trading, that involves finding high-quality, market-leading companies that will provide necessary goods and services for long periods of time, and holding on to them long enough to reap the benefits of their successes. This book will show you how surprisingly few companies meet those criteria for long-term success.

I believe the other part of that training is understanding the risks that never go away when you invest. One of the seldom-told secrets of investing is that even the most valued stocks in history have experienced times when their prices go down a long way. In my 30 years in the business I have come to view the market as a shark swimming noiselessly and dispassionately through ocean waters. When this shark attacks, it does so brutally and quickly, taking your arm with it without a glance back to see your reaction. While you can't plan your investing life based on worrying about a market shark attack, you always have to be aware that the predator is out there. That's what risk management is all about.

The shark has been active in the late '90s, swimming off with a lot of investors' appendages. It doesn't make the losses any easier to take, but I have the advantage of having seen a similar movie before. When I started in the market, I timed it to perfectly coincide with the last great prolonged market downturn, a period of time in the early '70s when stocks reached a point of irrelevance for most Americans.

It was a brutal period to be starting out as a stockbroker, but I must admit this last downturn is, in some ways, worse. As I mentioned in the opening here, the difference this time around is the overwhelmingly democratic pain it has caused to a larger group of investors. Never have so many fallen so hard for the dream of early retirement based on skyrocketing values. And the business press and investing community played a key role in the enticement that has disillusioned investors who believed they could trade stock certificates to easy riches.

My take-away from experience with downturns is the opposite of the conventional wisdom. Instead of scaring me off from investing in equities, I believe the downturns demonstrate how powerfully positive capitalism is. Over long enough periods of time, the market overcomes the downturns and rewards investors better than any other financial instrument. To me, the lesson is simple: The system works.

And, this time around, there are remarkable stories being written even as we fret about real problems of today. Advances in technology offer the promise of amazing improvements in our lives, ranging from genomic cures for cancer to smart appliances and high-tech inventory control. The companies that participate in these improvements will be the Microsofts,

Intels and Ciscos of the 21st century. Part of the fun of becoming a Citizen Investor is the search for these companies.

When people talk about investing, they talk a lot about emotions like fear, greed, and envy. In this book I will talk a lot about another, under-appreciated emotion: confidence. The confidence I'm talking about is an emotion experienced by those who have a solid strategy that involves a long-term goal. Think of Warren Buffett, the oracle of Omaha. He didn't get that lofty moniker by flinching every time the market hiccuped. He has invested with confidence for so long, many investors have stopped paying attention to how he has done it. I think it is time we paid homage to confidence as a timeless investing approach that transcends all gimmicks.

Oh, in this environment, you will hear about gimmicks. They come to you in the guise of investing methods that will make you feel better by reducing the risk of the market. Be aware of products that offer you "all the benefits of the market without the risk." When it comes to investing, risk never goes away. Only by taking risk can you reap the full rewards of the market. This book will show you how a successful retirement requires that you take full advantage of the market rewards.

As always, stocks are not for everyone. If you want instant gratification, you should turn elsewhere, as you should if you are using money you need today.

And, you may be wondering why a person who works for a full-service brokerage firm is preaching about self-sufficiency. I believe that while investing requires a partnership with an informed advisor, it is a distinct advantage to be dealing with informed customers. Despite what the on-line trading firms may say, I don't think you can do this all yourself. You will need outside advice, if only to save yourself from making decisions in a vacuum.

With all that in mind, I hope this book puts you in the position to consider taking responsibility for your own retirement and become a Citizen Investor. Let's get started.

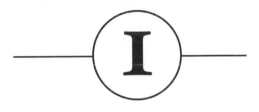

THE CITIZEN INVESTOR

HOW TO USE THE POWER OF DOMINANT COMPANIES TO BUILD A PORTFOLIO THAT WORKS

Kansas City, 1974

My father was a saver. If you lived through the Great Depression, you know what that means. You always set something aside for the hard times that could be around the corner. It's a great attribute, one we all could learn from.

Like most savers, my father was cautious. Back when my father first started putting money away, bank deposits were insured up to $10,000. So, my father would open an account at one bank, and once he had saved $10,000 he would promptly open an account at another so that all his money was federally insured.

As part of a lifetime of hard work, saving was a strategy he believed in and it formed one of the basic tenets of his life, but it had one flaw: He didn't plan on dying at age 62 with only a pension, Social Security, and those savings to fund my mother's standard of living.

After my father's death, my brother Paul (also in the financial services business) and I did some very sober reflecting and concluded that, without some kind of portfolio of stocks, my mother, who was just 50 when my father died, was going to have to watch her spending carefully.

To help my mother, Paul and I put together a basket of stocks made up mostly of blue-chip growth companies that had a history of steadily increasing sales and earnings, stocks that we thought would continue to appreciate in price over time and ease my mother's fears about having enough to live on.

And, you know what? It worked. Unlike some of my mother's friends who lost money in investing fads of the '70s and '80s—such as oil and gas income partnerships and yield-enhanced government bond funds—my mother had a fine retirement for the 22 years she lived beyond my father. I'm glad Paul and I designed the portfolio for her—and for me.

You see, despite my experience as a stockbroker, it wasn't until we put together a successful plan for my mother that my eyes were opened to what really works as an equity investment strategy for clients: buying not just good stocks, but those exceptional companies, and then holding on and letting time prove just how powerful an ally it can be.

It is one word, ownership, that forms the basis of this book; it is the cornerstone of becoming a Citizen Investor.

Annapolis, Md., October, 2002

It was another day of market free fall, not a great day to be telling a room full of panicky investors out East my story about how I became a Citizen Investor.

Before I went on, a silver-haired woman approached me, another one of the sea of faces I see when I give seminars on behalf of RBC Dain around the country.

"Are you giving the speech tonight?" she asked as I stood waiting for the branch manager of our office in the Maryland capital city.

"Yes, ma'am," I replied.

"My husband and I have to leave early," she said. "What kind of stocks are you going to be recommending?"

"Well, I really don't talk just about stocks," I said. "I talk about finding great companies and holding on to them once you do."

"So, you'll be saying that we should hold on to these stocks and, if we do, everything should be all right in the long term," she asked.

"You've got it," I said.

"Then we don't need to hear your speech," she said with a smile. "You're telling us what we already believe."

MEET THE CITIZEN INVESTOR

There are a great number of investors—male and female—who are just like that woman who spoke with me before my speech. I think of them as Citizen Investors, a breed of American whose savings have created the capital that has fueled the historic growth of this country. I have seen and talked to these investors in most cities where RBC Dain has an office. In Minneapolis, they are the ones who have smiled when I mention Medtronic. In Seattle, they have been investors in Microsoft. In Austin, Texas, they have been the buyers of Dell computers—and Dell stock.

These investors have traditionally found companies located in their backyards, known the employees and managers, many of whom may be their neighbors, and developed a strong understanding of these companies. Ownership of them is a natural motivation. In fact, they frequently add to their holdings of these firms on a regular basis, much as my father made steady contributions into his savings accounts.

With this kind of commitment to the companies, it's no surprise these investors usually don't think of selling their shares of these firms. They know firsthand that the people running these companies, and the products they produce, are strong enough to compete effectively and weather the inevitability of market declines. They have a strong faith that these companies are powerful, growing organisms, not trading tokens.

If there is any flaw in this strategy, it is that it can be too parochial, based only on companies close to home. And, in some cases, the allegiance to the companies has ignored flaws in their strategy. Even with the strongest companies, it doesn't pay to put all your money in just one or two.

But, the concept of finding companies you can believe in is what investment confidence is all about.

This book takes that idea one step further. It is about how you, as a Citizen Investor, can find the dominant companies across the country and create a portfolio of 13 to 20 stocks, a portfolio that has the potential to outperform a fund while offering the risk-spreading protection that comes from being diversified.

Now let me underscore something about this approach. This strategy is **not** about being passive and buying and holding through thick and thin. This is about becoming a passionate investor, or one who reads widely about the firms you invest in, getting enjoyment—and hopefully financial gains—from understanding their strategy and successes.

With the democratization of the financial markets, which is just a fancy way of saying for the first time in history it is a natural activity for everyone—not just the rich—to buy stocks, we all have the opportunity to become Citizen Investors, and it is probably a good thing to think about.

Here's why: If you have a defined-benefit pension that will provide a large part of your retirement income, you are now in the *minority* of American workers.

Most companies have turned to defined-contributions, the 401(k)-style plans in which the amount of the future benefit varies depending on investment earnings.

That would be fine if people were not living long enough to exhaust these funds, but the really scary statistic is this: If you live to be 65, your average life expectancy is another 18 years. That's 18 years of food, fuel, and housing that will have to be paid for from some source. And we know that source will not be primarily from Social Security, a system set up when few people lived to be 65. A 2001 Georgia State study found that prospective retirees need to be able to generate about 75 percent of their current income to maintain their standard of living in retirement, up from 63 percent of their income in 1997.

The conclusion from all of this is clear: For most of us, it's very likely that some level of ownership of stocks will be required to provide the returns needed to fund a retirement that will last us to age 83.

In effect, most of us should consider becoming Citizen Investors if we are going to have a retirement without overwhelming financial worries. The state of our future depends on the decisions we are making today. And, most people are ill-prepared, from a risk management perspective, to make those decisions.

The average investor with a saver's mentality is risk averse: they are concerned primarily about the return *of* their money and, only secondly, about the return *on* their money.

Bull markets are easy for this type of investor. When everything goes up, you don't have to worry about risk.

The irony is that risk is always present. That's what being an investor is all about: understanding and learning to live with the risk. The payoff in becoming a risk-tolerant investor is receiving a higher return than a savings account can bring.

I try to get this point across in the other part of my job that I haven't yet mentioned. As part of my duties as equity strategy director at RBC Dain, I play a talking head on TV. You know who we are, those people who appear on CNBC, CNNfn, and Bloomberg from trading floors who look like they know what they are talking about and can confidently give you stock ideas, pithy comments, and a catch-phrase about the day's market activity.

Yep, I am one of those. But if you saw how this process worked, you would find it remarkable that we can exude the confidence we do. When I'm going on TV, I get wired up with a mike and an earpiece to stand amid the maelstrom that is the RBC Capital Markets trading floor in Minneapolis. It's just me and the one-eyed bandit, a Sony video camera that acts as the stand-in for whomever I'm being interviewed by from a city hundreds or thousands of miles away. I've even been interviewed at the end of my working day by someone from Hong Kong who wanted my thoughts just as the Asian markets were about to open—a very weird concept.

Most of the time I can hear what the interviewer is saying and not hear my voice echoing up to the satellite or the squawk of a trade being delivered right behind me. But, there have also been times when I have been left trying to appear engaged while everything around me has fallen apart— literally, exploding television lights, members of the crew dropping things, you name it. A sense of humor has never been more necessary.

I tell you this to put the information you receive from the business press in perspective. Often, whatever you're seeing, hearing and reading is just one set of opinions, a snapshot of a long and involved movie. Acting on this kind of information is a risky proposition.

All in all, I see my role as giving the big picture regarding market and economic conditions in general while pointing out risks and rewards to those who can keep a long term time horizon. You may find it surprising that back during the market bubble of '99 and 2000, keeping perspective was a tough assignment. There were times when I was left saying I didn't understand the valuations and couldn't account for the prices some firms were trading at. Some of those appearances made me feel out of touch with the "new economy" that was leaving the "old economy" in the dust.

I'm not gloating at how things have changed; I just try to remember that guessing what the market or a stock will do in the course of a day is just that, a guess. And, when you're watching a breathless TV report about a hot stock, you should keep in mind that real trends from which you can profit are created over years, not hours. If you're entertained by business news, remember that's just what it is, entertainment, not investment counsel.

There are no quick fixes or easy answers although you can find people who will tell you there are.

No Shortcuts

Not surprisingly, as a result of the changes in the way companies fund our retirements, and the concerns most of us have about achieving our long-term goals, there are a lot of books and experts out there offering secrets to investing that will help you beat the market.

The idea that you only need to put your money in a sure-fire trading strategy or heating oil contracts and you will make returns far beyond any other investment can be very tempting. I'm sorry to say that when you are planning for your long-term financial future, you need to beware of any strategy based on secrets, tips, and tricks. You know the old saying, if it sounds too good to be true…

You need a strategy. And the one I have found that works best is searching out great companies, buying shares in them, and holding on.

I realize that what I am proposing will sound like heresy to the "buy-and-hold-is-dead" crowd who will point to the declines of the recent markets as an indication that this strategy will not work. And, they are right—if you use a year or two as your time horizon.

So, let me say this up front, this is not the book for you if you need to make short-term money or believe you are nimble enough to avoid declines and be positioned just ahead of significant stock moves. If this describes you, I wish you good luck (and suggest you get a professional involved if those are, indeed, your strategies).

But, if you look longer term, you will see that the companies that continue to prosper are almost always the same ones that have a history of prospering in the past. (What may surprise you is that there are so few of these dominant companies out there.)

One other word of warning. This approach is not intended to be used for all of your investments, or even for all of your retirement income. A wise investment plan would be diversified to include bonds as well as mutual funds and other professionally managed alternatives.

The Citizen Investor concept is designed to deal with a part of the equity holdings of your portfolio, money you will not need at any specific time. By using this approach, you will gain more financial knowledge than you have ever had. By reading annual reports, tracking companies' earnings, and paying attention to the products your companies produce, you will begin to understand why some firms dominate their sectors (with Wall Street rewarding them as a result). You will be applying those backyard investing skills to a larger portfolio that goes far beyond your town.

In other words, this book will **not** provide you with a list of stocks you should invest in. The examples in this book are just that, examples, which demonstrate the qualities of exceptional companies in the past. You should use this book to find your own firms, firms you know and understand that will form the basis of your investments. The dominant companies of the future remain undiscovered. The aim of this book is to provide you with the means to find them.

GET RICH SLOW

In a sense, this is an anti-investing book. Its secret is that there is no secret. Becoming a Citizen Investor is not rocket science. Simply put, you need to find companies that dominate their sectors, have strong products and innovative managements. Buy them, and pay attention to them, and you will create an investment portfolio that has the potential to give you more confidence than any other can provide. I can't state strongly enough the powerful sense of confidence derived from owning companies.

This investment approach is not about renting stocks or trading certificates, watching CNBC, CNNfn, and Bloomberg for every angle and ultimately being depressed by short-term results. It is about ownership. And just like owning a restaurant, gas station, or a beautiful piece of land, it is in owning something of value that long-term wealth has been built for centuries.

Nothing has given me more confidence than owning good companies that have steady earnings, effective strategies, and a base of loyal customers who believe in their products. I can write about this feeling, but you can only get this sense from doing it. When you begin to feel the confidence and responsibility of being an owner of successful companies, you will have become a Citizen Investor.

Let's see how you can do that.

THE POWER
OF BULLDOGS

WHERE THIS IDEA CAME FROM; WHY IT WORKS

So, how do you become a Citizen Investor?

It starts with finding the right companies, what I have taken to calling "bulldogs." A bulldog is an industry leader; a world-class competitor; a solid profit-making company driven by innovation, productivity, and superior leadership. In this book, you'll see me use "dominant companies" and "bulldogs" interchangeably. They mean the same thing: companies that produce consistent earnings growth and whose success is recognized by Wall Street.

(The first time I heard the term "bulldog" was in the '90s. James Moltz, chief investment officer of New York investment firm C.J. Lawrence, used it to create an image of companies that embody strength and tenacity. The metaphor has stuck with me.)

So, with that by way of background, let me introduce you to a couple of historical bulldogs. These two are in the same industry. In a decade of amazing performance, the stock price of each grew more than 9,000%! That means that if you had invested $10,000 in either at the beginning of the decade, and held on to the stock, 10 years later your shares would have been worth more than $900,000—even if you never bought another share. (These are pretty unusual, even for dominant companies—don't expect this kind of performance from your stocks.)

As I said in the last chapter, as Director of Equity Strategy for RBC Dain Rauscher, I speak to large groups of investors, and potential investors, about a dozen times a month. When I start discussing these two remarkable bulldogs, most of the people in the audience assume that I am talking about technology stocks, which isn't surprising. Convinced they are right, they throw out some obvious names—Microsoft, Yahoo, Intel, and Sun Microsystems.

When I tell the folks in the audience that they are way off, that the two bulldogs I am describing aren't high-tech firms, but companies that substantially outperformed them, the next assumption they make is that these bulldogs must lead some obscure industry they never knew existed. Say, a manufacturer of an auto part or a firm that makes a component of something found in every home. Wrong again. Not only do investors recognize the industry when I tell them, most have shopped at one or both of the companies. It's pretty hard to avoid electronics retailers.

The bulldogs are Circuit City and Best Buy, two firms with prominent locations in every major city that turned in their phenomenal performance in different decades.

If you bought shares of Circuit City in 1980, the value of that stock appreciated 9,287% by 1990. That means a $10,000 investment would have turned into slightly less than $1 million ($928,700 to be exact) 10 years later.

If you, in your role as a Citizen Investor, put $10,000 into Best Buy in 1990, your shares grew 9,376% (and became worth $937,600) by the time you opened your champagne to celebrate the dawning of the new millennium (and your good fortune in investing in Best Buy 10 years before).

You want to invest in bulldogs: an industry leader; a world-class competitor; a dominant profit-making company driven by innovation, productivity, and superior leadership that you can reasonably expect will grow faster than the market as a whole for an extended period of time.

I tell this story about these two bulldogs to steer investors away from the dangerous belief that the only way to create wealth in the stock market is to bet on high-tech companies, act quickly on the advice of TV analysts, and/or attempt the "buy low/sell high" market timing gambit.

Yes, as we will talk about in detail starting in the next chapter, being a Citizen Investor—someone who searches out bulldogs and holds on to them through the inevitable market ups and downs—requires patience and discipline, but the pay-off is a winning strategy that is independent of emotion, hot tips and the short-term whims of the market. (By the way, this approach is tax efficient as well since your gains most often would be taxed at the long-term capital gains rate as opposed to ordinary income!)

The boring reality of the stock market is that investors build wealth by buying and holding on to the stock of solid companies for several years. The success of this investment approach underscores the difference between owning a company and trading stock certificates: Owners carefully select bulldog companies in growth industries and remain patient through good times and bad—through Bull and Bear markets—while traders try to time the market by guessing which direction a stock will go. Even for the pros, timing is a dangerous game. In a volatile market like the one we've been experiencing the last few years, it's suicidal—and unnecessary. Investors can create wealth with a lot less risk by owning bulldog companies. Note the difference between being fully invested and missing even the 10 best days over a ten-year period, in the chart below.

Trying to Time the Market Can Be Costly December 31, 1991–December 31, 2002		
Period of Investment	Average Annual Total Return	Growth of $10,000
Fully Invested	10.65%	$27,526
Missed the 10 Best Days	5.99%	$17,887
Missed the 20 Best Days	2.63%	$12,968
Missed the 30 Best Days	-0.08%	$9,920
Missed the 40 Best Days	-2.48%	$7,782
Source: Bloomberg. The stock market is represented by the Standard & Poor's 500 Index.		

THE POWER OF OWNERSHIP

I've appreciated the power of ownership since I was a boy growing up in Prairie Village, Kansas, a suburb of Kansas City. There must have been 85 kids within shouting range of my house, any number of whom were ready for a game of baseball or a trek to the local swimming pool on a hot summer day.

My father was a Renaissance guy: an artist who worked with oils, as well as a sculptor and singer. During the Depression, he ran a vaudeville group in Chicago called

"Professor Cheer and the Cheer-Ups," but his stage career ended abruptly when he contracted tuberculosis. He spent a year and a half in a tiny apartment getting treatment, which at that time meant a drug delivered by needle several times a day into the rib cage. His buddies helped keep him alive by bringing back food from the soup lines.

As part of his recovery, doctors suggested he try building up his body through physical labor in a warmer climate. He moved to California to work in the fruit fields. He returned to Kansas City as a strong and healthy 35-year-old, and found a job as an office boy at an insurance company. Two years later, he was a vice president.

My mother's first career choice was artistic as well, although her dreams would also be unfulfilled. She grew up on a Kansas farm, one of eight children. In high school she was offered an art scholarship to the University of Kansas but had to turn it down because she couldn't afford the "extra" things, like having enough money for sheets to put on her dorm room bed. She worked as a handmaiden to wealthy young women, saving enough money to go to secretarial school. That landed her a job at the insurance company where she met my father.

My parents' story reflects an era where harsh reality overcame the endless optimism of the Roaring '20s, where saving every penny became the only balm for the nagging fear that we could suffer through another Depression. Survivors of hard times, my father and mother gave my two brothers and me a safe and happy world. We exemplified the nuclear family. Dad worked. Mom took care of the family. We shared a strong sense of community and tradition, including Sunday dinners after attending the Episcopal church.

Back then, I remember admiring the new Oldsmobiles the well-to-do people drove to church and wondering what they were doing differently from us. It was then that I began to understand the concept of wealth through ownership. The children of wealthy families had fathers who owned car dealerships or local businesses. They were the ones who had nice houses, speedboats in the driveway, and summer cabins. It took me 20 years in this business to learn that the concept of ownership, when applied to investments, is even more powerful than I imagined as a child.

Here's how I came to that conclusion. In 1990, I had to write a speech about what was important to investors. By this point in my career, I had learned that the market is very efficient over the long term—that stocks end up trading where they should—but terribly inefficient short term. This led me to conclude that any investment you make should have at least a three- to five-year time horizon, meaning no matter what, you should plan to hold on to a stock you buy for three to five years at the very least. My idea was that you would buy shares in a stock at an attractive valuation and then hold on as increasing earnings drew attention to the stock, eventually driving up the price.

So, investing for the long term became one of the key points in my speech—and it remains one of my fundamental beliefs today. If you can't stand that idea, if every half-point move in the stock price either makes you elated or depressed, then a bulldog portfolio is not right for you. If you have that kind of sensitivity to the marketplace, you're probably better off utilizing mutual funds or finding a money manager, one in whose ability to trade successfully you have faith, and hire him or her.

Now, I may be wrong, but despite all the inherent emotional pressure to buy and sell all the time—triggered by financial media, coupled with a volatile market—my experience is that most investors are like my mother was, confident in buying good companies and keeping them. They like the simplicity of holding on to good investments for the long term.

Of course, that led back then—when I was writing the speech—and it leads today to an obvious question: What are the best investments for the longer term?

That question takes me full circle.

Where It All Began

I got into this business in 1971. Fresh out of college with a degree in Business Administration, I had tried my hand at all kinds of selling. My first job was at Pfizer as a detail man. That meant I called on doctors and pharmacists and introduced new drugs or new applications for existing drugs. It was a good job. It helped me understand selling. And it helped me understand how to build relationships with people. I think I was reasonably good at portraying what the company wanted. But they were moving me all over the Midwest, and I felt that I would like to stay in one place, so I took a job with Olivetti selling office equipment on pure commission. That's where I probably learned the most about selling, and it was selling old-fashioned, dinosaur-type equipment like accounting machines.

But even though I did well in both jobs, neither one felt right. I had friends who worked for brokerage firms, and while I didn't understand a word they said about the markets, P/E ratios, puts and calls, and butterfly straddles, everything about the way they talked about their jobs appealed to me.

I liked the idea of being able to pick and choose among products that are best for a particular client. And financial services is one of the few businesses where you can do that. You can tailor a portfolio for customers using appropriate commitments to stocks, bonds, mutual funds, CDs, and insurance. I thought the idea of being a broker was very interesting because it would be selling—something I liked— without having to move all over the place, and you could concentrate on offering what was best for the client. It seemed to be exactly what I was looking for.

So in 1971, toward the end of a bull market—one fueled by growing consumerism and a war economy—I started as a stockbroker trainee at a small Kansas City firm called H.O. Peet and Company. My timing, from a personal point of view, could not have been worse. The Vietnam War had masked the fact that productivity gains were largely missing. There wasn't much innovation. Our smokestack economy relied heavily on a stable relationship between supply and demand and the availability of cheap fossil fuels. When the war ended and an oil crisis boosted fuel costs, the economy stalled. Stock prices plummeted. We entered a full-blown bear market, with stock prices falling dramatically over 630 days during 1973 and 1974.

The early '70s were one of the worst times in stock market history. Investors watched helplessly as the value of their holdings dropped month after month with no end in sight. It felt like slow-motion torture. I remember meeting with my clients and telling them to hold on to their investments because the market had hit bottom, only to watch it decline further. Every once in awhile I'd suggest buying stock in a promising company but it, too, would flounder. Things got so bad that I had one client, a farmer in Lawrence, Kansas, who said sympathetically, "Phil, I'll send you a check every month. I just don't need your ideas."

To give you an idea of how little regard people had for the stock market at the time, in 1974 a taxi registration medallion in New York City cost more than a seat on the New York Stock Exchange. Really. The medallion cost $37,000 while the seat was $34,000. The medallion probably seemed like a better buy.

What we didn't realize back then was that great companies were emerging. These firms were tremendous profit generators that were only beginning to create shareholder value.

During the '70s, I had hunted for innovative new companies in the hope that they could give my clients impressive returns by "getting in on the ground floor." I figured that was the way people could grow truly wealthy.

Two things helped change my mind.

First, the approach didn't work. Whatever approach you take to investing has to endure over time. And my strategy certainly wasn't successful during the bear market of the early '70s.

Second, after Kidder Peabody bought H.O. Peet, I met Dick Kimball. Dick was head of equity (stock) strategy, and one of the first things he did after I met him was look at the stocks I was recommending to my clients.

We had pretty good research at my old firm, so we would come up with recommendations for companies we thought would be huge winners, firms that would come out of nowhere and surprise on the upside.

Dick looked at my book—the listing of the stocks I was recommending—shook his head and said, "Gosh, you're tough."

"What do you mean?"

"Well, you are recommending all these stocks that are real aggressive. If you're right, it's great, but more often than not you're going to be wrong, and that hurts your relationship with your clients, and you have to go out and get more clients."

Kimball said, "Phil, why don't you learn how to sell more conservative stocks, ones that you think are going to grow consistently over time, rather than constantly swinging for the fences?"

That was exactly the approach Kimball took, and he did a very professional job for our clients. If I could be half as good as he was, and he was great, I'd do fine.

If you talk to anybody who was at Kidder between 1979 and 1982, they will tell you that Kimball was just a master. He's probably the single greatest influence in my career. I took his idea of finding and recommending good, solid companies with a history of growing their sales and earnings, firms that had staying power, and built off it. My whole idea of conservatism through ownership can be traced back to Kimball.

THE PROOF IS IN THE NUMBERS

The most convincing evidence that I was on to something was a *Forbes* article that changed my mind forever about swinging for the fences all the time.

As the list below shows, the '80s was the decade of consumer industries, from companies that manufactured products to the retailers that sold them. We shopped at these stores and bought these products without giving much thought to the steady growth in sales and earnings from the companies behind them. The following returns convinced me that these were the kinds of companies in which people should have been investing.

The 10-year summary opened my eyes to the power of owning solid businesses—and to the money that could be made if you do. Today, New York taxi medallions go for less than $200,000. A seat on the NYSE just commanded $1.825 million.

When I finally crystallized my thoughts for a speech in 1990, I emphasized that the best businesses for longer-term investment are solid growth companies, the bulldogs that lead their industries.

Best Companies of the 1980s	
Company	Stock Return for the Decade
Circuit City Stores	9287%
Hasbro	6606%
Limited	6357%
Mark IV Industries	6257%
Marion Laboratories	3973%
Wal-Mart Stores	3767%
Gap	3719%
Dillard Department Stores	3705%
Shaw Industries	3554%
Tyson Foods	3317%
Home Depot	3147%
MCI Communications	2788%
Hannaford Brothers	2722%
Berkshire Hathaway	2495%
Savannah Foods	2447%
CDI	2391%
State Street Boston	2364%
Price Company	2273%
Cooper Tires & Rubber	2248%
Toys 'R' Us	2176%
Source: Forbes, January 8, 1990.	

Note: This performance is cited for illustrative purposes only. Past performance is no guarantee of future results, and this reference should not be construed as a recommendation to buy or sell any of the listed securities. Returns cited do not include fees or costs associated with the investment.

Having established my theme, I started to elaborate. I said investors need to understand that buying stock in a bulldog means owning a piece of that company. If you don't know why you own it, you're in trouble. But if you do, and you have truly identified a bulldog, investing becomes not only more profitable, but more tranquil.

Here's why. For a Citizen Investor who acts like an owner, the daily fluctuations in a business' value mean little within the context of the company's long-term potential. A successful business owner doesn't pick up the phone or a calculator every day to find out what his or her business is worth. *That's not how owners behave.*

Owners—of businesses or bulldogs—track indicators of financial performance (revenue, profits, margins, etc.) with strategic goals in mind. They analyze the competition, listen to their customers, and plan ways to grow their businesses. They understand that a down day or a bad quarter requires context. It requires them to ask questions such as: Has this happened before? What caused the decline? Has the fundamental business model changed, or is this just one of the short-term dips that periodically happens for reasons beyond the owner's control?

These are exactly the sorts of questions I ask as an investor. When I think of owning part of a bulldog, I think of a shop owner on Main Street. The shop owner invests in a business he or she believes will return a profit over the long term. A winning investor's focus, likewise, should be on a company's financial performance compared to long-term expectations, not on short-term stock price performance.

You Can Do Better

The alternative to being a Citizen Investor is, of course, to become the owner of a small business. While I admire the patience and tenacity that building a business requires, frankly, there's a better way for the less tenacious of us to be an owner and build wealth, one that avoids the relentless stress of working long hours trying to satisfy fickle customers, managing inventory, meeting payrolls, and handling all the details that can make or break a business.

The alternative? Become a Citizen Investor with all the rights and privileges that go with that.

Here's a personal example. In 1993 an investment analyst told me, as he was telling all our clients, I was missing a great opportunity. I should own stock in Medtronic. Medtronic is a Minneapolis company that is one of the world's leading medical technology firms. It makes a host of devices that help treat cardiovascular disease, diabetes, and other diseases.

Although I had two kids in college at the time, I scraped together enough money to buy 100 shares of Medtronic, which was then trading for $58.50 a share. Today, about 10 years later, through stock splits, those 100 shares have become 1600 worth about $50 each, as I write. That's about a 13-fold return on my investment. There are very few startups that could deliver such impressive returns. Since I invested in it in 1993, its annual earnings have grown at more than 28% a year on average. To put that into perspective, of the 6,000 companies that *Forbes* tracks for its list of top companies, only 143 grew annual earnings at 15% or better for the '80s.

Show me a company with an established track record of producing above-average revenue and earnings growth and I'll show you the makings of a bulldog. Once you find one, buy shares and hold on.

> *The fact is companies that are truly great—ones that steadily grow sales and earnings—are rare, and if you're lucky enough to own such a firm, selling it, even if its stock has already doubled or tripled in price, can be one of the worst decisions you'll ever make.*

What makes a true bulldog? By my definition, bulldogs grow earnings at least 10 to 15% a year and I would love to own companies that can do that for 10 years or more. As we have just seen, there are very few that can. That's why to be even considered as a potential bulldog, a company will have to have produced that growth for five consecutive years. (We will discuss all this in detail in Chapter 7.)

There is a simple reason I place so much emphasis on profits. Earnings growth typically acts as a catalyst for shareholder value. That is a fancy way of saying that once investors find a company that consistently turns in above-average earnings growth, they want to own a piece of it. That demand makes the bulldog's stock price go up.

Since the market price doesn't tell us anything about the future, I want to buy and hold stocks in industry-leading, profit-making bulldogs. Over the long term, earnings will drive the stock price higher and you will profit handsomely.

Now, I realize that your investment dollars could grow much faster if you picked **THE** right aggressive tech stock at exactly the right moment, but the risks of losing your money are high if you employ that strategy.

Consider a short list of the casualties that once looked like sure things: E*Toys, Pets.com, Mortgage.com, and Dr. Koop.com. What serious investor is willing to stake his or her future on a company whose stock price is determined largely by sentiment—is this particular tech stock in vogue at the moment—especially when that investor has the choice of going with industry leaders with proven exceptional earnings?

Serious investing isn't about making "good trades"; it's about creating wealth while intelligently managing risk to hopefully provide a return higher than the one produced by the market as a whole.

That sounds boring on the surface. But think about it this way: Over the last 76 years, the stock market has produced annualized returns that have averaged about 10% a year. At 10%, it takes more than seven years for your money to double. If you can achieve a 13% return, it doubles much quicker—that's 33% faster. All of a sudden, those returns don't look so boring.

In the chapters ahead we will not only talk about how to find these bulldogs but also the mind-set you must have to see this investment approach through. But for now, let me just foreshadow the topics we will be discussing. They all involve the need to:

◆ *Be disciplined.* You need to adopt a strategy and stick to it in good times and bad. Part of that discipline will call for you to be diversified at all times (stocks, bonds, real estate, and cash). I don't know about you, but I'm not willing to bet the house on one poker hand, even if I think the cards I'm holding are likely to win.

◆ *Understand the (low) cost of ownership.* Another reason
to own companies, rather than trade stocks, is because
ownership is cheaper. Not only do investors avoid
transaction costs by buying and holding on to bulldog
companies, they also eliminate the tax bite that comes
if you sell a stock less than a year after you bought it. If
you sell within 12 months, any gains—the IRS rightly
refers to them as "short-term" gains—are taxed as
ordinary income under the current law. Even the
government wants you to be a long-term investor.
That's why there are long-term capital gains rates and
tax-sheltered plans like IRAs. Having a clear
understanding of all the costs of ownership helps
investors pocket a greater portion of their investment
returns.

◆ *Be patient; you need to make time your ally.* Everybody
wants to beat the Street. Very few succeed—and that
includes investment professionals. A study of 100 large
pension funds found that 89 of them lost money when
they tried to "time" the market. It is no better for
money managers. Depending on the period surveyed,
some 70% to 80% of the people who manage mutual
funds fail to beat a specific benchmark, such as the
performance of the S&P 500, in a given year. Trying to
time the market is a loser's game. According to a study

by the University of California-Davis, the more decisions an investor makes, the more likely he or she will lose money. To the serious investor, what happens in the market today is not that important. Creating wealth is a marathon, not a sprint.

◆ *Be willing to put in the work to find the companies that are likely to become bulldogs.* (Don't worry, I've devoted an entire section, Chapter 5, to showing you how to find them.)

◆ *Set realistic expectations.* Although it's true that the best performing companies deliver phenomenal returns, it's also true that they are exceptions to a typical stock's performance. I suppose you could "realistically" expect a 1,000% annual return if you put all your investment dollars into a company you knew would grow like Best Buy of the '90s or Circuit City of the '80s, but nobody knows who the next Best Buy or Circuit City might be or even if they will emerge. I believe it's reasonable to expect a bulldog portfolio over time to outperform the broader market.

◆ *Manage risk.* Traders who try to time the market accept different risks than most investors. Buffeted by minute-to-minute financial news, they fret about exactly which second they should buy or sell. In contrast, serious investors build wealth by sticking to their long-term plans. They understand that the greatest risk to a bulldog stock is not the daily fluctuations in its price but the deterioration of the core business that made it a bulldog in the first place. An investor manages this risk by knowing why he or she bought the bulldog initially, then monitoring its performance to make sure that purchase maintains its pedigree.

I believe as a Citizen Investor you can apply these fundamentals to make better investment decisions, in part because the approach is so focused. It's simple because it allows you to ignore the daily noise on business TV and radio. Instead, you can focus on finding—and monitoring—the performance of dominant companies. Rather than being overwhelmed by an expanding universe of stock possibilities, you can cut through the clutter to the very few bulldogs that lead their industries. You don't have to outguess the unguessable fluctuations of the stock market.

By rewarding patience over activity and discipline over impulse, the simple philosophy of buying and holding on to bulldogs takes full advantage of the market's efficiency at valuing earnings growth for the long term. You can create wealth by owning stock in a diversified list of bulldog companies for long periods of time.

How This Is Different Than Value Investing

Let me spend a minute clearing up a potential misconception. Before moving on, I want to make sure we're clear about the difference between value and bulldog investing.

Dominant firms are winning companies with real earnings. They grow in value because the most significant driver of stock prices over time is earnings growth. Earnings are a catalyst for driving stock prices higher (or lower.) Better yet, they're a catalyst we can understand and monitor. It is easy to see when earnings rise (or fall).

So the conclusion is clear: Finding companies that can consistently grow earnings is a successful formula for wealth creation.

While I've been known to buy a good value stock from time to time, my focus is on bulldogs, which are quintessentially growth companies. Value investors pick stocks that are selling for less than they're worth, or as celebrated value investor Warren Buffett puts it, selling for less than their "intrinsic business value."

To me, assessing value is much harder than spotting growth. I understand growth. I think any investor is able to find and monitor businesses that can grow at above-average rates for extended periods of time. Buying growth companies is a simple approach that doesn't rely on too many complicated factors for success.

I admire value investors like Buffett who have the proven ability to pluck underappreciated stocks from the pile and hold on to them until they gain broader support. But I realize that not every investor has the resources or the expertise with financial statements to do the research necessary to determine a good value buy.

For me, it's harder to trust value investing to produce consistent returns because you're relying on other investors to discover the same hidden value in a company that you think you've uncovered. Those companies may not enjoy the quarterly catalyst of higher sales and earnings that spark price performance.

Instead, you're waiting for something to develop, for an unknown catalyst to spark interest in the stock.

So value investors need to rely on two variables in order to have success:

◆ They have to excel at both analyzing information, and

◆ They then need to wait patiently for others to reach the same conclusions about the worth of the company they have invested in.

But as a growth investor, I still look for value plays. Here's an historical example of what I look for, a company like ChevronTexaco Corporation.

ChevronTexaco has not been a growth story, but it has been a poster child for strong companies in underappreciated sectors. ChevronTexaco has been one of those oil patch firms that has been a truly integrated energy company. It has had its hands in oil and gas exploration, production, refining, and marketing, as well as power and chemical manufacturing.

Following the merger of Chevron and Texaco in October of 2000, the company has exceeded its projected merger synergies by $400 million and has maintained production growth of 2.5% to 3% a year. Ultimately, it has the potential to end up being a very powerful single firm that could be more attractive than the other international energy companies it competes with.

The market decline of 2001–2002 positioned ChevronTexaco as a bargain not only compared to some of its competitors, but to the market as a whole.

As a story for investors, ChevronTexaco has been as straightforward as they come:

- ◆ solid management;
- ◆ accelerating merger synergies;
- ◆ an improving return on capital employed; and
- ◆ a strong demand for its products.

On top of this, ChevronTexaco has paid a dividend of 3.8%. To me, all factors considered, this has been a stock that merits a closer look.

NOW IS THE RIGHT TIME

When clients ask when they should buy bulldog stocks, I always tell them, "Right now!"

For a bulldog investor, there's no time like the present to own shares in dominant companies.

Want proof? Consider this:

The stock market hits its yearly low only one day each year. The same is true for its yearly high. The odds of buying at the low or high are about one in 250 (about the number of days during the year you can buy or sell stocks). The table below shows what would have happened if you had been the luckiest person on the planet, investing $1,000 in the S&P 500 every year on the one day the market hit bottom. It also reveals what you would have made if you had the worst timing, investing the same amount on the one day each year when the market hit its peak.

As the table shows, making investments and staying invested is far more important than the timing of the investment. And that is true even if you use professionals to help you.

Best Day			Worst Day		
Market Low	Cumulative Contribution	Year-End Value	Market High	Cumulative Contribution	Year-End Value
Dec '02	$43,000	$701,218	Dec '02	$43,000	$623,006
Dec '01	$42,000	$913,527	Dec '01	$42,000	$811,987
Dec '00	$41,000	$1,049,150	Dec '00	$41,000	$932,822
Dec '99	$40,000	$1,166,356	Dec '99	$40,000	$1,037,128
Dec '98	$39,000	$974,797	Dec '98	$39,000	$866,866
Dec '97	$38,000	$768,502	Dec '97	$38,000	$683,578
Dec '96	$37,000	$585,591	Dec '96	$37,000	$521,032
Dec '95	$36,000	$485,891	Dec '95	$36,000	$432,433
Dec '94	$35,000	$361,302	Dec '94	$35,000	$321,708
Jan '93	$34,000	$365,880	Dec '93	$34,000	$325,771
Apr '92	$33,000	$331,710	Dec '92	$33,000	$294,959
Jan '91	$32,000	$307,761	Dec '91	$32,000	$273,235
Oct '90	$31,000	$235,676	Jul '90	$31,000	$208,525
Jan '89	$30,000	$242,611	Oct '89	$30,000	$213,919
Jan '88	$29,000	$183,910	Oct '88	$29,000	$161,623
Dec '87	$28,000	$157,148	Aug '87	$28,000	$137,761
Jan '86	$27,000	$148,471	Dec '86	$27,000	$129,476
Jan '85	$26,000	$124,315	Dec '85	$26,000	$108,087
Jul '84	$25,000	$93,810	Nov '84	$25,000	$81,283
Jan '83	$24,000	$87,455	Oct '83	$24,000	$75,541
Aug '82	$23,000	$70,551	Nov '82	$23,000	$60,723
Sep '81	$22,000	$57,482	Jan '81	$22,000	$49,262

Source: New Standard & Poor's

Best Day			Worst Day		
Market Low	Cumulative Contribution	Year-End Value	Market High	Cumulative Contribution	Year-End Value
Mar '80	$21,000	$59,393	Nov '80	$21,000	$50,679
Feb '79	$20,000	$44,083	Oct '79	$20,000	$37,491
Mar '78	$19,000	$36,343	Sep '78	$19,000	$30,730
Nov '77	$18,000	$33,161	Jan '77	$18,000	$27,973
Jan '76	$17,000	$34,646	Sep '76	$17,000	$29,104
Jan '75	$16,000	$27,021	Jul '75	$16,000	$22,623
Oct '74	$15,000	$18,782	Jan '74	$15,000	$15,728
Dec '73	$14,000	$24,071	Jan '73	$14,000	$20,243
Jan '72	$13,000	$26,985	Dec '72	$13,000	$22,684
Nov '71	$12,000	$21,722	Apr '71	$12,000	$18,208
May '70	$11,000	$18,019	Jan '70	$11,000	$15,046
Dec '69	$10,000	$16,084	May '69	$10,000	$13,484
Mar '68	$9,000	$16,427	Nov '68	$9,000	$13,727
Jan '67	$8,000	$13,725	Sep '67	$8,000	$11,461
Oct '66	$7,000	$10,096	Feb '66	$7,000	$8,415
Jun '65	$6,000	$9,985	Nov '65	$6,000	$8,352
Jan '64	$5,000	$7,855	Nov '64	$5,000	$6,511
Jan '63	$4,000	$5,761	Dec '63	$4,000	$4,720
Jun '62	$3,000	$3,696	Jan '62	$3,000	$3,002
Jan '61	$2,000	$2,696	Dec '61	$2,000	$2,277
Sep '60	$1,000	$1,120	Jan '60	$1,000	$993
Average Annual Total Return: 10.6%			Average Annual Total Return: 10.2%		

Note: This performance is cited for illustrative purposes only. Past performance is no guarantee of future results, and this reference should not be construed as a recommendation to buy or sell any of the listed securities. Returns cited do not include fees or costs associated with the investment.

As Charles Ellis, author of *Investment Policy: Winning the Loser's Game* pointed out:

"Just as there are old pilots and bold pilots, there are no old, bold pilots; likewise, there are no investors who have achieved recurring successes in market timing. Decisions that are driven by greed or fear are usually wrong, usually late, and very unlikely to be reversed correctly. Particularly with real money, don't even consider trying to outguess the market or outmaneuver the professionals to "sell high" and "buy low." You'll fail, perhaps disastrously."

With all the media pressure to buy or sell based on today's news, it's important to keep the pitfalls of timing in mind. As study after study has shown, and as the tables prove, if you're going to invest in stocks, now is the best time to do it—and it doesn't matter when "now" is. It's silly to wait for what you hope will be a better time. Don't time the market. Invest in bulldogs today and put them to work for you.

GETTING OUT

Okay, that takes care of when to buy, but clients also ask when to sell. Normally, you don't ever want to sell a good stock.

The problem I have with sell disciplines—strategies that teach when to get rid of a stock—is a philosophical one. You

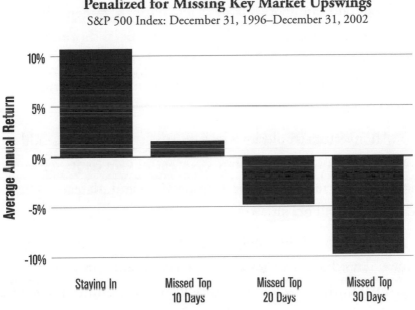

In-and-Out Investors:
Penalized for Missing Key Market Upswings
S&P 500 Index: December 31, 1996–December 31, 2002

Source: Bloomberg calculations by Van Kampen Investments, Inc.

can't be an owner and sell. Once you sell, by definition, you are no longer an owner.

Owners and Citizen Investors understand the ebb and flow of a business. If the business model is sound, they recognize a dip in earnings, or a decline in sales, as a temporary aberration. Owners don't panic when adversity strikes, and neither should the Citizen Investor.

A lot of people crave the comfort of stop-limit orders, automatically selling their stock when its value drops below a set point. That comfort comes with a high cost. Most people fail to buy before the stock resumes its ascent, and if it's a bulldog, odds are that (re)ascent *will* happen. When a bulldog goes down in price, it doesn't mean it has been shot in the head and is dying. With increasing market turbulence, many stocks can swing as much as 50% **every year**. Be patient. Trust the discipline.

All investors would love to own stocks that grow steadily month after month, year after year. Serious investors separate fantasy from reality by expecting declines and plateaus. The down days will occur.

The Citizen Investor approach helps me through those down days. First, I've got at least 13 companies in my personal portfolio—and that should be the minimum size of a bulldog portfolio—one that's losing half its value may ruin my appetite, but it won't kill me or my overall returns. Second, by remembering that the average stock can lose 50% of its value in a year, I don't panic when a bulldog does the same. Cisco's stock has lost half its value *three times* in the last seven years. A stop limit order would have kicked investors out of Cisco, a company that ended up with the highest 10-year return in history.

By limiting your scope to great businesses, you're still going to be wrong, but you'll be wrong less often. You're still going to have underperforming stocks, which is why we are talking about owning at least a baker's dozen, instead of just one. But as long as you stick to a discipline of owning stock in 13 or more dominant companies in growing industries, I've found that you will more than make up for the times you're wrong.

And you *will* be wrong. AT&T had all the makings of a bulldog in May 1999; one could see great opportunity in the company's vision of being a single source for customers' telecommunication needs. Local and long-distance telephone, cable, Internet, and wireless would all be provided by AT&T. One bill each month. One big company meeting all of a customer's needs at a reasonable price. We liked the vision.

To achieve its vision, AT&T spent a lot of money buying cable companies. It depended on its long-distance business to pay for the acquisitions, but just after the start of the new century, that revenue source began to shrink. Price cutting, already prevalent, ramped up to the point where AT&T was forced to offer long-distance service for less than 10 cents a minute. Some people are now paying as little as a nickel. When AT&T started announcing that earnings from long-distance were not what they expected, a holder should have questioned his or her assumptions and reevaluated the company's business model. Instead, many waited.

At the time, the research coming out of Wall Street remained positive on AT&T. Value analysis indicated that AT&T's component parts were worth a total of $60 a share, and many thought its one-stop business model made it more valuable than its individual pieces. It was selling for $40. In this example, it had been bought at $61 a year earlier and many had reason to hope it would bounce back; it was understandable to remain optimistic despite the signs that its business model was deteriorating. Six months later, only when it became apparent that its business model was no longer viable—when it was apparent that AT&T was no longer a bulldog—it was time to sell. For $20 a share.

It could have been—and obviously should have been—sold earlier, but I don't think you sell just because a company's share price falls. I think you sell because your forward-looking assumptions about a company's business model prove wrong. You don't write the epitaph for a company when it still has a visionary position and no signs of losing it.

The rest of the story is that AT&T's broadband business, the part of the business that seemed so promising, was bought by Comcast, a firm that is trying to take advantage of all the groundwork AT&T laid. The deal places Comcast in the forefront of every emerging digital media technology of the cable industry: digital cable services, video-on-demand, high-speed broadband, and other high-tech services.

Comcast appears positioned well to do what AT&T couldn't. But, whether Comcast can execute so ambitious a plan is a question that only time will answer. The story is still compelling, and we are watching it closely.

I'm an optimist by nature, having decided early in my career that pessimism would not serve me well in the financial services field. I don't know many successful people, including investors, who are pessimists. That doesn't mean I don't expect some bumps in the road. Warren Buffett is a lot smarter than I am and even he's had a couple of bad years. (Remember when people were saying he was over the hill because he was not buying dot.coms?) To me, being optimistic when it comes to your finances means trusting an investment discipline. The roots of such confidence stem from having an investment discipline you believe in, one that has proven itself in up markets and down. How you create such a strategy is the subject of our next chapter.

DISCIPLINE

D o you remember the "dartboard" stock-picking contest that *The Wall Street Journal* used to run? Even if you don't, it is pretty easy to understand how it worked. About once a month, the editors of *The Journal* would invite a group of experts to pick their favorite stocks. Then a *Journal* reporter threw darts at random at the stock tables, and whatever stocks they landed on became the *Journal's* portfolio. Six months later, they compared to see who did better.

You know the punch line. Many times, it seems, the dart won, generating a higher return than those stocks picked by the professionals.

But there is a difference between entertainment and serious investing. Throwing darts may work once in a while, but as a long-term strategy for building wealth, it leaves a lot to be desired.

Why You Need a Discipline

If stock market returns were totally random, then throwing darts would be as good an approach to investing as any.

But if you look back historically at the stock market, invariably you get to a point where you begin to recognize that returns over time are not random. They are fairly constant.

If you review all the data compiled by Ibbotson and Associates, a Chicago-based financial research firm, you'll see that, overall, the stock market has returned about 10% a year on average going back to 1926. Sure, some years are a lot better, and some years—like the ones we experienced in the beginning of this millennium   the returns are actually negative, but over the last 75-plus years, the returns have averaged about 10% annually.

Jeremy Siegel, a finance professor at the University of Pennsylvania's Wharton School of Business, has gone back to the 1800s and tracked returns from the early 19th century until today, and his numbers are consistent with Ibbotson's. Siegel's research in *Stocks for the Long Run* shows that the stock markets have returned about 10% a year on average for almost 200 years.

A History of Inflation-Beating Returns
The Value of $1,000 Invested from 1926–2002

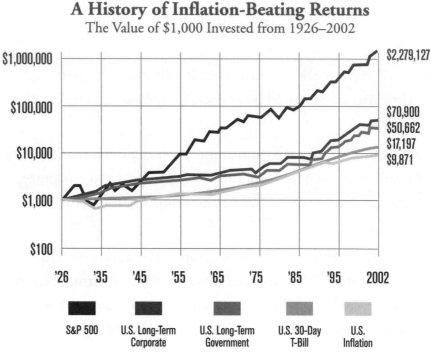

Source: Ibbotson Associates, Chicago.

Note: This performance is cited for illustrative purposes only. Past performance is no guarantee of future results, and this reference should not be construed as a recommendation to buy or sell any of the listed securities. Returns cited do not include fees or costs associated with the investment.

As you can see, the returns are pretty consistent, and since they are, taking a random approach to investing probably isn't going to help you much.

You need a plan, a discipline.

Historically, there have been two major disciplines people have used to help keep them in the game: growth investing and value investing.

Let's take them one at a time.

Growth is exactly what it sounds like. Investors who follow this approach look for companies that consistently deliver *above average* earnings gains. They may look at other things as well, factors such as return on equity and revenue growth, but their real focus in determining whether or not they buy a stock is on a company's earnings. Do they believe that the company in question will grow its earnings faster than the market as a whole? If the answer is yes and the valuation is reasonable, then they buy.

The second popular discipline is value. And this is where the focus is principally on the real worth of a company. What is its intrinsic value? Is that value fairly reflected in the stock price? If it's not, if the company is substantially undervalued versus its tangible assets, you buy.

This is the way Warren Buffett invests. He finds companies that are trading substantially below their intrinsic value, buys them, and holds on until the overall market discovers what he already knows and drives up the share price to what the company is actually worth. Buffett is not only the quintessential value investor, in 2002 *Forbes* said he was also the second richest man in the U.S. (In case you are wondering, Microsoft's Bill Gates was the first.)

Contrarians make up a subset of the value school of investing.

If you are a contrarian, it means you're buying things that nobody else likes. A great example of the contrarian approach is the people who buy the Dogs of the Dow.

You may have heard of this trading strategy. Every late November or early December, the believers in this strategy buy the five or ten stocks that have been the worst performing members of the Dow Jones Industrial Average,[1] over the last 12 months. They are buying into a universe of companies that very rarely goes bankrupt, as a rule is conservative, and could best be described as a very visible herd of "elephants" that tend to survive and endure. They are buying these stocks when they are out of favor. These stocks are, as Wall Street-types would say, not efficiently priced. That is, for whatever reason, they are trading below where they should be.

---

[1] The 30 stocks that make up the Dow Jones Industrial Average are: Alcoa, American Express, AT&T, Boeing, Caterpillar, Citigroup, Coca-Cola, Disney, DuPont, Eastman Kodak, Exxon Mobil, General Electric, General Motors, Hewlett Packard, Home Depot, Honeywell, J.P. Morgan Bank, Intel, International Business Machines, International Paper, Johnson & Johnson, JP Morgan Bank, McDonald's, Microsoft, Minnesota Mining and Manufacturing (3M), Philip Morris, Merck, Procter and Gamble, SBC Communications, United Technologies, and Wal-Mart.

As you can see, there are a lot fewer "industrials" in the Dow Jones Industrial Average than there used to be. The editors at Dow Jones, which publishes **The Wall Street Journal** and **Barron's,** revise the list periodically to reflect overall changes in the U.S. economy.

The market has priced them as if they're going out of business, and then, lo and behold, they come back because they're big businesses and big businesses tend to rise along with the overall economy. The result? You end up being invested in a group of stocks that operationally tend to bounce back and do well, after they have been beaten down for a while. That's why the Dogs of the Dow approach works.

As you can see, Dogs of the Dow is a short-term value strategy, one that requires changing the stocks you hold each year. This is in direct contrast to the Citizen Investor strategy where you buy stocks in good companies, ideally at an attractive price, and hold on to them for the long term, i.e., three to five years. The stocks I am talking about are not temporarily out of favor, but are dominant firms in their sectors that produce strong returns for long periods of time. Bulldogs are literally a different breed than Dogs of the Dow.

With bulldogs, the price you pay for them originally is far less important than their growth potential.

So both growth and value are each a discipline you could follow, and it's important to have a discipline—and be disciplined—when it comes to investing. If you don't, you'll be subject to the whims of the market and how it prices stocks, and you'll be tempted to react to every twist and turn. Without a discipline, people tend to focus purely on the emotional side of investing, and when emotion enters, it can really hurt your performance.

What We Are Talking About Here

When we say you need a discipline, it sounds like we are pronouncing a harsh sentence. But, really, what the word "discipline" represents is rules to live by if you are going to own stocks. And those rules are often what are missing when most people start to think about investing. Most of us don't have an overall guiding philosophy behind how we buy and sell shares. But then again, that shouldn't come as a surprise. The whole concept of investing is relatively new to most of us.

We had always been, like my father, a nation of savers, and it has only been in the last 25 years or so—primarily as a result of the shift away from defined benefit plans (pensions) to defined-contribution plans (401ks, 403bs, SEPs, Keoghs)—that most of us have become investors.

The problem is many people started seriously investing at a time—the '80s and '90s—when it didn't take any real discipline to succeed. The adage "everyone's a genius in a bull market" was never more appropriate. We were in the midst of a great bull run, and just about everything went up in price. People became reward-oriented in the '80s and '90s; that is, they bought a stock and immediately expected it to soar in price. It is only now that they are learning the kind of discipline that is needed.

To put the 2000–'02 bear market in perspective, it has outlasted the '73–'74 decline by more than 370 days while producing a slightly lesser decline in the value of stocks—48% versus 46% for the S&P 500. The total loss of value was an estimated $7 trillion this time around. That kind of decline can be hard on any investor, but it is especially punishing to the uninitiated participant who lacks a strategy for his or her investments.

As the last few years have taught us, you've got to understand how to manage risk. Having a discipline allows you to do that.

Your alternatives—relying on everything from tips to market timing—won't permit you to do that. Since you already know this, we will only take a minute or two to review why this is the case.

The trouble with tips is basically twofold:

1. They sound great, but it is very, very hard to check their validity, and

2. They only focus on part of the investing equation: you get the buy advice, but rarely do you get a tip about when to sell.

You may get the tip from a friend. You may get the tip on CNBC, CNNfn, Bloomberg, or Fox News. And by its very nature, it's enticing and exciting. It's normally given in a sort of hushed, whispered tone.

I think what's crazy is when you go out and bet a lot of money on a long-shot stock. That's gambling. Investing isn't gambling. It's about effectively managing your assets for retirement and your other financial goals.

Need further proof that tips don't work? Look at two of the very best investors, Peter Lynch and Warren Buffett (guys who have produced 20% gains over the decades). These guys don't buy on tips. Neither should you.

I Heard It through the Grapevine; Timing the Market

You could listen to rumors. Rumors are kind of like tips except sometimes you get a little bit more. But, unfortunately, often you get a lot less.

The best example of a rumor is "advice" like, "you want to buy XYZ Co. because they are a likely takeover candidate." Or, to put it even more enticingly, "You want to buy the stock because the valuation is good, the company is good, and oh, by the way, they may get bought out."

The difficulty here, of course, is what exactly are you going to do in the event they don't get bought out? You are stuck owning a stock that you have bought for the wrong reason.

With regard to market timing, there are legions of studies that have been conducted—my favorites were done at Stanford and University of Michigan Business Schools—and they always show the same thing: Market timing doesn't work.

Let me give just one example. Stanford Professor William F. Sharpe came to this amazing conclusion about the possibility of market timing successfully:

"(A) manager who attempts to time the market must be right roughly three out of four times merely to match the overall performances of his competitors who don't."

Sharpe found there were two reasons for this. The money manager:

◆ Will often have his or her funds in cash equivalents in good market years, sacrificing the higher returns stocks provide during such periods; and

◆ Will incur transaction costs in making switches into and out of stocks.

Beyond the numbers, the studies reveal all kinds of interesting things. For example, if you missed only a few of the biggest days in the marketplace, your return went down pretty dramatically for the year.

But perhaps the most important finding was this: It is very difficult to make money with this approach as a discipline.

You can understand, intuitively, why that is the case. When you are talking about pure market timing, you are talking about going totally into the market—that is, putting every cent you have into stocks—and then going totally out of stocks, and then coming back in and then out, and then in...

In other words, you're trying to avoid all pain of the downside, and gain all benefit of the upside. But, according to the research, you need to be right three-quarters of the time to make any money with this approach. And statistically, we've never had any .750 hitters in baseball—or investing.

So, as alluring as it is to think that there's a psychic hotline or a technical tool or a black box computer program that can master the concept of market timing, there isn't one.

Common sense tells you market timing is a lot like building a perpetual-motion machine—something that is impossible to do.

There are two other things that have proved to me market timing is truly a bad idea. The first involves the market conditions we have gone through in recent years. It has been easy to know the last couple of years that it's raining outside, that we had a condition that was not good for stocks. So it's been simple to know to get out. The challenge is when do you get back in? The opportunity to be wrong on when you reenter the market is pretty strong.

And the second and final piece is this. If you look at the market's performance over the last 129 years, a Stanford University study will show you that in 95 of those calendar years—or 74% of the time—stocks have gone up.

I walk away from this saying that if the market goes up most of the time, why would you try to time it at all? That's especially true when you realize that if the market goes up 10% a year on average, it has to be doing better than 10% in its up years, to offset the times when it goes down. Since that is the case, all that timing does is get you out of an asset that goes up most of the time and leaves you open to missing out on any upside bias.

To me, timing is very much a loser's game. And, by timing, I am talking about day traders, too.

And if you trade frequently, you are basically involved in a variation of market timing.

We've created a whole nation of people that were day trading during the big Internet bubble. In retrospect, I think it is pretty easy to see how that came about. But as these people learned the hard way, day trading is a whole lot harder than searching for bulldogs.

WINNING BY NOT LOSING

When it comes to trading—what most people think of when they think of investing—your success is defined by the number of mistakes you make. The fewer the better. And it seems clear to me, the more decisions you make, the more chances you have of being wrong. So those multiple decisions we just talked about—market timing, frequent trading, and the like—just increase the chances you will make a mistake.

We have seen that stocks, overall, normally go up, and making decisions that will take you frequently out of the market, just give you more opportunities to miss the move upward.

Those are pretty compelling reasons to hold on. Here's one more. My final argument against making frequent moves is the expense involved. It costs 1–2% of the value of a stock to make a roundtrip trade—one where you buy and then (eventually) sell shares in the same company—whether you are using a full-service broker or are trading on-line. Just think what happens if you do that multiple times during the year, on an asset that has traditionally returned 10% annually. You are eating up potential returns in transaction costs. And even if you are paying less, trades still reduce your potential returns.

And then, of course, you have taxes to deal with. Certainly, long-term capital gains rates benefit patient long-term owners.

That is no small point. If you are an active trader and are lucky enough to produce a gain under the current law, you will pay up to 35% in income taxes (depending on what tax bracket you are in) on whatever you make, since short-term gains are taxed as ordinary income. Hold the stock for more than a year, and you pay no more than 15% on your profits.

When you add it all up, not being disciplined costs you money. You need a discipline. And the one I like is buying—and holding on to—bulldog stocks!

The Power of the Hungry Bulldog

To me, a bulldog is a company that tends to dominate its industry. The more dominant bulldogs can grow earnings over extended periods of time, and the best bulldogs produce strong revenue and earnings growth regardless of what's going on in the economy. Most tech stocks, as we have learned, are cyclical. Medical stocks are not.

For example, if a doctor prescribes a cholesterol drug or a defibrillator or a pacemaker, you're normally not going to wait for the economy to get better to go get the prescription filled, purchase the device you need, or schedule surgery. There's a pretty strong motivation to go ahead and do what needs to be done to turn your life around. That's why stocks in companies that make medical devices, orthopedics—companies that make replacement hips and knees just to identify one area— and pharmaceuticals tend to do pretty well on the earnings line. And they normally have pretty high growth rates over time, and they tend to endure.

In the case of Medtronic, a Minneapolis firm that makes medical devices, the decision to sell has been pretty much the wrong decision for the last 20 years.

So I like companies like that, and I also tend to find bulldogs among the food companies. You've got to eat and drink, no matter what is happening in the economy.

With bulldogs you don't worry too much about timing— be it when you buy their product, as or as we talked about earlier, their stocks.

But, again, let me stress something that I said back in Chapter 1. Investing in bulldogs is not an all-or-nothing approach. I think owning bulldogs should be a major component of an investment plan that also includes mutual funds with some exposure to small, mid-cap, value and foreign stocks, and, of course, bonds.

But that said, I think bulldogs should be a part of your investment portfolio. (We will discuss in detail in Chapter 9 what the equity portion of your portfolio should look like.) Whether they are growth bulldogs—as most bulldogs are—or value bulldogs, these types of dominant companies should be part of your equity holdings.

WHEN DO YOU SELL?

Not only do I think you should own bulldogs, I think you should hold on to them once you do. With a really good bulldog like a Dell or MBNA, I'd almost never sell all of it. Although I might want to make a partial sale to put the money in new investments.

The only time when I might sell a larger portion of a bulldog is when it is a technology company like Cisco. There I might sell a piece of it if its valuation became bloated.

Cisco is one of those stocks where if you had invested $10,000 at the right time, you could literally have ended up with $12 million. At the bottom, it fell from trading at $82 or $83 a share in 1999–2000 to a low of around $10 in 2001.

But even at the bottom, a $10,000 investment was worth something on the order of $3 million. It was a huge home run.

Ironically, this is the problem with technology stocks; they can move up much more quickly than equities in other industries, and they can fall further and far faster.

This argues for a slight variation of the standard bulldog rule, which is to buy and basically hold on forever. The variation? Buy and be prepared to sell a *piece* of a tech bulldog.

When do you sell? And how much? One discipline I like is when the stock is trading at a very high multiple of its sales rate. Cisco, at one point, was trading at 15 times sales. When it reached that point, I should have sold some.

Whenever I see anything close to that kind of valuation or even an exorbitant evaluation, I'm probably going to take some money off the table in the future, and I think you have to.

But the key message here is that it's the rare company that can grow earnings at an above-average rate for a long period of time, say five or ten years. There are no more than a handful of companies that can do it. In the '80s, fewer than 1% of the companies grew earnings at 15% for the decade. In the '90s, when it seems every company did well, it was still no more than 5% to 8% of the total universe of publicly traded firms—only one in 12 at best, and one in 20 at worst. Those are the companies you want to own.

What I Didn't Say

Now let me stress that what I just said is different than "stay away from tech." Far from it. A lot of these tech bulldogs like Cisco, Intel, and Microsoft have been gaining market share in a really tough environment in recent years, even though they have not been showing great earnings and revenue gains. Their balance sheets have shown that they have been as strong as battleships. Each company has had billions of dollars in cash. Historically, when the economy has turned around following periods of decline, companies with strong balance sheets and strong market positions do well.

Still, they have been *tech* bulldogs. And so that means selling to lock in some of the gains during their bull runs. My sense is that when these stocks do get overvalued, you want to lighten up a little bit, but always keep a core position in a tech bulldog. Nobody I know is smart enough to buy them at the bottom or be in them just before they trade up again.

However, I would probably sell some. I never thought I would say that. My world has changed a lot. The market's changed it, at least when it comes to technology-based bulldogs.

Still I would say there's a pretty strong argument to be made for being a Citizen Investor and owning dominant businesses. The big buyers of a product or service like to do business with an efficient provider who can give them both good service and provide ancillary products at a reasonable price. And it seems more and more that scale is important on a global basis.

So that would mean the ultimate bulldog would be:

- ✓ a global competitor,
- ✓ that has a solid balance sheet, and
- ✓ produces at a very competitive price a product or service that is in high demand.

That is, of course, on top of the things we talked about before—the company is steadily growing sales, earnings, and market share.

All these factors make up the profile of a bulldog. And if you own bulldogs, you eliminate the risk of trying to time the market. You don't have to be a great trader to own them.

Looking for a bulldog? Look for a visible company with financials that are compelling. (More on this in Chapter 5, Searching for Bulldogs.)

IMPLEMENTING YOUR DISCIPLINE

Knowing the strategy you are going to follow is one thing, knowing how to put it into practice is something else. This is where an approach like dollar cost averaging comes in.

The whole concept of dollar cost averaging, where you invest a fixed amount of money—say $300—into the market at regular intervals—once a month—is hugely powerful.

The technique of moving money into investments on a regular basis has been proven to mitigate the effects of short-term volatility in the stock market. The result is that you will frequently end up paying less per share.

Some hypothetical numbers will show how this works.

Dollar Cost Averaging: By the Numbers			
Month	Regular Investment	Share Price	Shares Acquired
January	$300	$10	30
February	$300	$5	60
March	$300	$10	30
April	$300	$25	12
May	$300	$15	20
Total	$1,500	*	152

*The average share price over that time was $13. Yet, by using dollar averaging, you would have paid $9.87 for your shares. The numbers above reflect a hypothetical scenario and are for illustrative purposes only.

So, you buy at an average lower price. That's good. Plus, using this approach forces you to invest on a regular basis, and that may be even better.

As the example shows, this is a great way to invest.

Dollar cost averaging works well if you are buying shares in a good growth fund, a good value fund or even an S&P index fund. And I might use it until I had somewhere around a combined $30,000 to $50,000 to invest in individual bulldogs. (You are probably going to need that much because, as we have talked about before, you are going to want to own a minimum of 13 bulldogs and as many as 20, and you will want to have a representative position in each.)

TIME, TIME, TIME IS ON YOUR SIDE (YES, IT IS)

Is there a certain time horizon for the Citizen Investor approach to work?

Yes.

My best guess is that you need a minimum of three to five years. That's the length of the typical economic cycle, and normally you can see how a business model does if you track it over that amount of time.

But that means you have to think about how you are
going to use this approach. Bulldogs are great as a long-term
investing approach. But as it comes time to pay for a financial
commitment—your daughter's wedding; that vacation cabin
you have always dreamed of—no investing approach that
relies on investing in the stock market is a good idea. Long
term, stocks go up, but in the short term they can bounce
around all over the place, and you can't afford a 10% drop in
the value of your child's college fund a month before Junior is
supposed to go off to school. Bursars are not going to push
back the tuition deadline until the market comes back.

The Proof Is in the Pudding

Okay, I've convinced you. You've decided to be
disciplined. What do you do? Well, if you like the idea of
bulldogs, you would put together a portfolio of somewhere
between 13 and 20 stocks.

Why 13 to 20? Because all the research in the field says
once you have bought 13 stocks spread out across a number of
industries, you have the potential for pretty good
diversification, and adding the 14th stock doesn't help you
much.

I can't say you will have the same amount of market risk
with 13 as you would if you bought a Wilshire 5000 index

fund. But the actuarial risk data on the topic shows that a diversified 13-stock large-cap portfolio provides roughly 90% of the diversification of the market at large.

So, 13 would be the minimum number of stocks to have and 15 to 20 stocks strike me as not a bad number. Any more than that and you reach a point where the number of stocks you have is hard to follow, and that defeats the purpose of a bulldog portfolio.

Now, once you have put together your portfolio, while you should always review your account statements thoroughly, you probably don't want to check prices frequently— remember, you are not a trader, but an owner.

But as an owner, you want to focus on financial guideposts. To me, that's the key. The real distinction between an investor, someone who is a dispassionate trader, and someone who views the market with their emotions, is how he or she approaches the market. And as I said before, you want to look at your stock holdings as a business owner would.

And, as we have talked about, owners don't calculate the value of their business daily. Instead, they look at the financials. They want to know: Are sales good? Is it reasonable for us to expect sales to continue to grow? They wonder, "What's a reasonable growth rate? How are my costs and how do they impact my margins? Are my margins secure? Can they be enhanced over time? What is the health of my enterprise?"

One easy way to track all this is to read the company's annual report and quarterly results. In any good annual report, the chairperson or president, will tell you what a reasonable growth expectation is for the company's revenue and earnings lines. He or she will also present overall themes regarding what is going on at the company today and where he or she expects the firm to be in the future. And then your job, as an owner of the business, is to pay attention each quarter to see how the company is doing against the benchmarks it has set for itself.

Can you really expect people to do this kind of homework, you may ask. If you want to be a Citizen Investor, you will.

You want to own companies that do what they say they're going to do. And there just aren't that many great managements out there. Paying attention to financial guideposts and understanding the business you have invested in helps keep you in the game.

Again, you want to act like an owner. In hard times, do you see the Ford family wanting to sell their Ford Motor stock? No. The reason? People get wealthy because they own something. With the democratization of capitalism, there is powerful opportunity to create wealth through ownership. Unfortunately, the average person has gotten caught up in trading certificates, not owning companies.

The *Wall Street Journal* recently reported on the trend of investors turning to franchises instead of stocks. According to the *Journal*, the out-of-pocket cost for a franchise can range from $9,000 for Tax Centers of America to $35,000 for Great Clips to $175,000 or more for a Krispy Kreme doughnut shop.

On top of that, franchisees often take out small-business loans for several times their cash investment to finance equipment and real estate. For example, excluding land, it stills take $1.1 million to open a Krispy Kreme.

The returns can be good—if you work hard, have the right product, and benefit from a little luck. But cashing out can be difficult and you have to deal with issues like personnel problems, insurance and long hours at a job.

My sense is that 100 shares of a bulldog company is probably a better buy than becoming a franchisee of McDonald's or Krispy Kreme from the standpoint of owning a business. You can get higher returns for doing a heck of lot less work.

Keeping all this in mind is how I try not to get emotionally involved in the ups and downs of the market. I try to recognize that I am an owner of companies that exist in a marketplace where stocks have always delivered a reasonable return over time.

It helps me stay focused. I am disciplined enough to invest in bulldogs, and investing in bulldogs gives me the discipline I need.

STOCK
OWNERSHIP

There are two words in the title of this chapter: "Stock" and "Ownership," and not surprisingly people want to concentrate on the first one.

"What stocks should I buy?"

"What is going to appreciate the most?"

"How soon will my money double or triple?"

Wanting answers to all these questions is definitely human nature, so I am not surprised when people give all their attention to the first word in the chapter title.

But let me start with the second—ownership.

The word implies certain things:

◆ You paid your hard-earned money to purchase something, in this case a stock. It wasn't a gift. You didn't find it. You worked in order to be able to purchase it. And now you own it. It's yours.

◆ Implicit in your decision to buy is that you spent some time thinking about it before you pulled the trigger. Unless they have much more money than they need, people think about what they are going to purchase before they actually plunk down their (hard-earned) money.

◆ There is pride in ownership. Did you ever wash a car you rented on vacation or during a business trip? Probably not. How about the car you drive every day? A different story, right?

All these factors come into play when you are talking about becoming a Citizen Investor.

They don't if you are trying to time the market.

If you are buying shares of a company at $10 convinced you are going to get out once it hits $11—something you hope will occur during the next day or two—you don't think in terms of ownership, only trading. That's fine, if that is the way you want to approach the market.

But it isn't the path I'd take.

I believe in being a Citizen Investor, an owner, which means I:

a) Buy a stock after giving the purchase serious thought, and

b) Plan to hold on to my purchase for a while.

If you take this approach it means you will want to start out by looking for stocks that you will be happy to hold for a while, stocks you expect will endure.

That means you may want to begin in places like health care, specifically medical, pharmaceutical, or orthopedic devices.

Other areas that show a lot of potential growth may be a little more defensive—meaning they do particularly well when the rest of the stock market is falling. They could include beverage and food companies, the more efficient the better. And if you search hard enough, you can usually find myriad companies that are likely to grow in terms of revenue and market share.

Ultimately, it doesn't matter what specific companies you invest in. Basically, you want to own a good business. That's the number one thing.

You want to find a good firm and hold on.

This is exactly the approach people who create companies take. When a business, such as brokerage or computers, falls out of favor, do you hear about founders like Bill Gates or Michael Dell wanting to sell their ownership? You don't. It would be an indication that they have lost faith.

Over a long period of time, if you choose well—and you aren't going to pick all of them well—you can create wealth by thinking like an owner. Having an ownership stake, which is of course what happens when you own shares in a company, can create wealth as a company's revenues and profits grow, and the firm pays its shareholders dividends, and the stock price rises.

To me, stock ownership is owning a piece of the U.S. economy. You are trying to buy an asset that will grow over time, one that will protect you against the ravages of inflation and the inevitable downturns that we will have.

You are trying to find good businesses to own. Again, you are not going to be able to pick them all perfectly, but the good ones you discover should make up for the ones that don't quite pass muster over the long haul.

Thanks to the democratization of capitalism, where more and more Americans own stocks, this is the first period in our history where the little guy has had a chance to latch on to a growing stream of either dividends, or stock appreciation, or both, that can create wealth over time. MIT economist James Poterba wrote in "The Rise of the Equity Culture" that stock ownership had risen 75% from 1989 to 1998, reaching a peak of 51.8% of all U.S. households. When I talk about the Citizen Investor, that is what I am talking about: wealth through ownership.

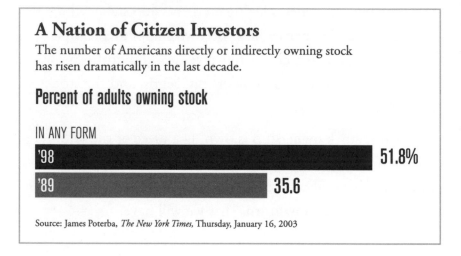

A Nation of Citizen Investors

The number of Americans directly or indirectly owning stock has risen dramatically in the last decade.

Percent of adults owning stock

IN ANY FORM

'98   51.8%

'89   35.6

Source: James Poterba, *The New York Times*, Thursday, January 16, 2003

This is no small point. Look at any list of wealthy people, such as the *Forbes* 400. What you will see is that there are two primary places where their money comes from. First, the people on the list are like Bill Gates and Leslie Wexner, men and women who founded—and remain substantial shareholders in—companies such as Microsoft and The Limited.

The second source? It's inherited wealth. And from whom did members of the Walton family, for example, inherit their money? Sam Walton, the man who founded Wal-Mart.

Owning companies is truly a way to become part of this path to wealth.

Now that, of course, is true over the long term. As I mentioned when we were talking about Gates and Dell a page back, stocks of these companies—like all companies—can go down, and that means the owners' net worth falls along with it. But I'd say in that case it's a question of losing the battle and winning the war.

Periodically, the market goes down. Yet, as we have seen over the last 129 years, 74% of the time, the market has gone up. (Specifically, the biggest 500 stocks have gone up.) That means there is pretty positive momentum to the upside. Even factoring in the 26% of the time the market has gone down, the overall return for stocks is in excess of 10% a year.

Here's the takeaway message: The long-term rewards of the market are permanent, and the short-term losses are temporary.

So I would view Michael Dell's loss, or Bill Ford's loss, as a short-term problem. Over the long haul, their most valuable asset—their shares in their respective companies—will probably gain in value.

I think we are at a great moment in our history where the little guy can own companies instead of trying to trade stocks. Institutional investors are paid to trade. They are rewarded by buying and hopefully achieving a short-term gain and then moving on to the next stock.

That may work for them, but I think there is something lost in doing that for the rest of us.

Look at Warren Buffett, who is a value investor. He said that watching him invest is like watching paint dry. And he is right. There is not a lot of excitement associated with his approach to investing. He owns the companies he buys for 5, 10 and 20 years. He's not hooking up with an Internet trading croupier. And he is not trading every day, every other day, or even once a month. So, from an excitement point of view, he is absolutely right. Watching him invest really is like watching paint dry.

But he is very, very rich. So, something about this approach is working for him.

Given Buffett's success, why aren't more people following his approach? My sense of the individuals who are either trading a lot or, conversely, are staying out of the market—that is, they don't own anything and never will—is that they are missing two things:

1. a general understanding of risk management tools that individuals can use, and/or

2. the power over time that comes from the ownership of really good companies.

Let's touch on both points briefly. One common reason people give for not investing in stocks is that they are "too risky." But here is something to keep in mind. People who say that tend to be thinking about those particular days when stocks have declined significantly.

However, think about what we just talked about, in discussing that 74% of the time the market has gone up. Even factoring for the major declines recorded in 1929, 1987, the bear market of 1973–74, and the bursting of the tech bubble in 2000, stocks on average have returned slightly more than 10% a year. Short and simply, stocks remain the most rewarding long-term financial asset.

As for the power of ownership, that is simple. Good solid companies that consistently grow their earnings are rewarded by Wall Street. Investors who own these companies do well.

THE WRONG END OF THE TELESCOPE

A problem, of course, can come from moving too far the other way, in expecting too much from ownership.

This issue crystallized for me in 1990 when *Forbes* came out with a list of the best-performing companies of the '80s. It showed, for example, that $10,000 in Wal-Mart on January 2, 1980, had become worth $780,000 by the end of the decade. The article came out at a time when stocks were becoming very popular, thanks to the growth of defined-contribution plans, and people started to think that returns of 20% to 30% a year were their birthright.

But if you are looking for the stellar gains we saw in the '90s, you are probably looking at the wrong thing, or at the very least expecting far too much.

The primary goal in ownership should be obtaining an asset that can repeatedly and dependably grow in revenues, earnings, and dividends; and if that asset—shares in a company in this case—pays dividends to shareholders, so much the better. Solid, dependable returns should be your goal, and not the terrific numbers of the '80s and into the '90s.

My point is that in the '80s and '90s—and today, too, for that matter—there are very few companies that had the ability to grow for an extended period of time at above-average rates. There was a popular article in *Fortune* during the summer of 2001 called "The 15% Delusion" that pointed out there are only a handful of companies that can grow earnings at a rate of 15% a year every year for 20 years. You are trying to find some of them. You won't find all of them.

Given that, set your sights a bit lower. Try to find great businesses that can grow at a 10%-plus rate on a dependable basis and hold on to them for long periods of time. This is the proven way to create wealth over long periods.

How are you going to find these solid performers? I think that if you stick with relatively large, visible companies, ones that have scale on a globally competitive basis, you have a good shot. That is at least the place to start.

To be sure, you're going to be wrong from time to time, but over long periods true, high-quality growth businesses will bear fruit and deliver the kind of wealth creation we talked about (and, in the process, help offset the stocks that you were wrong about).

A recent research report by Standard & Poors refines the evidence supporting ownership of high-quality companies. The report provides strong evidence that, as in the past, buying and holding premium-quality companies is likely to be a winning strategy. The report tracks stocks rated A+ (the S&P's highest rating) from 1986 to 2002 and finds that those stocks compounded at 12.3% annually vs. 10.8% for the S&P 500. All A-rated (A+, A and A- stocks) beat all B-rated issues by a 2.4% margin.

WHAT SHOULD A CITIZEN INVESTOR CONCENTRATE ON?

OK, you have started searching among potential bulldogs; what exactly should you look for?

I think there are four things to concentrate on. You want to know:

1. Can the business maintain its leadership position in its industry? That means you want to focus on the potential bulldog's revenues and market share. Obviously, you want these numbers to be going up and ideally to be going up faster than the industry as a whole.

2. Is it profitable? Can it become more so?

3. Is the growth sustainable?

4. What does the balance sheet look like? You don't want to own companies that are highly leveraged. I would say you only want to look at firms that have no more than 30 percent of capitalization in debt. The ideal is to try to find companies that are innovative, companies that spend significant amounts on research and development to keep ahead of the competition without taking on much—if any—debt.

Now, as the last couple of years have shown, companies will put out numbers that will put them in the best possible light. But my sense is that going forward there is going to be a commonality of interests between putting the best face on things and putting out numbers that people can trust. In any event, paying attention to the financial guideposts is critical.

If you do, and the numbers are solid, and the company has good answers to the four questions we posed above, you'll know the reasons to hold on to it.

Doing all this research will make the investment process less emotional, and you can make better decisions.

Let me give you an example. Think back to when President and Mrs. Clinton were talking about how they were going to change health care. There were some huge opportunities created when the large institutional money managers dumped health care stocks, in anticipation of severe reforms in the industry.

People who owned health care stocks, and who knew what was going on, not only held on to what they had, they bought more and were handsomely rewarded for withdrawing emotion from their investment decisions. This was a true case where ownership paid off.

A similar thing has been going on recently. Wall Street institutions have been worried about pending patent expirations of prescription drugs that the pharmaceutical industry has in the pipeline and the outcome of a presidential drug benefit plan for the elderly. As a result, the whole drug group has been on its knees. We'll see what happens three to five years from now, but we know from history that some of these great growth companies from time to time get irrationally cheap, based on emotion-driven selling. And when that happens the market has tended not to value the long-term worth of the franchise. Those moments have represented huge buying opportunities.

DRIVING HOME THE POINT

I'm not sure that people truly understand the distinction between owning businesses and trading (stock) certificates.

For me the best way to draw it is to return to an idea we mentioned before in passing. Think of owning shares of a company like being an entrepreneur, someone who owns a business.

Most people who own a company look at the key numbers that govern their business—revenue and earnings growth, margins, etc.—convinced that if they focus on the key variables, the value of the business will take care of itself. This is exactly the approach you should take as a shareholder.

As I pointed out in Chapter 2, most entrepreneurs don't focus on the price, or the value of their enterprise. They don't keep a running ledger of how much their business is worth and update it on a daily basis. They focus on the financial characteristics of their business: Is the top line—their company's revenues—growing? Is it likely to continue to grow? Are the margins secure, and if they are, can they be enhanced? How dependable is the growth rate? Can it, too, be increased over time? These are the questions an entrepreneur asks about his or her business. Instead of focusing on the daily fluctuations in the stock price, these are exactly the same questions you should be asking as a shareholder. You are an owner, just like the entrepreneur.

Now the analogy isn't perfect. Entrepreneurs have direct control over the asset—their companies—and shareholders, like you and I, only have a minimal say over the direction of the companies they own. People point that out and then ask, "How can I tell exactly how well my asset is doing, and more important, how can I expect it to be doing in the future?"

Good questions. I always tell these people to turn to the annual report of the bulldog they own. That is always the starting point. Keep your eye out for newspaper and magazine stories about the company's quarterly earnings—basically, read everything you can about the company to get a well-rounded opinion of the health of the enterprise to which you have committed your hard-earned cash.

Once you have that information, you want to own companies that do what they say they are going to do and accomplish those financial goals. As in life, surrounding yourself with quality people of high integrity has its rewards.

Owners don't check the value of their business every day, and neither should Citizen Investors. Focusing too much on daily swings can really hurt you. Checking the value of your holdings monthly is reasonable, although most of us do it far more frequently than that. But the reality is the market is not really efficient, short term, in valuing some bulldogs, so the only thing checking more frequently will do is drive you nuts.

What Kind of Citizen Investor Are You?

People tend to like the answer about reading the chief executive's letter, but then they go back to their original point and ask: "If you only own 100 shares of the 500 million that a company has outstanding, are you still really an owner?"

Yes.

You will benefit if the company does grow its enterprise, and its earnings increase as a result. As other people learn of the company's solid performance, they'll want to buy the stock, and that increased demand will send the share price higher. If the company pays dividends, the dividends will grow along with the firm's rising earnings, and you will definitely benefit over time. And should the company decide to plow the money it would have paid in dividends back into the business, that will probably cause the business to expand and drive the stock price higher, as sales and earnings increase as a result of the additional investment. Additionally, bulldogs can split their shares when they grow quickly, and you can end up having a rather sizable number of shares.

For example, I bought 200 shares of Cisco in the early to mid-'90s, and of course it's fallen quite a bit recently. Still, there were a number of splits before the decline began, and I believe I now have close to 3,600 shares, and my cost basis is under one dollar.

Now even though the stock has declined somewhat, it still trades significantly higher than the dollar I paid for it, on a split-adjusted basis, so I have a pretty significant asset. And Cisco has been a company with as much as $21 billion in cash, no debt, and even through these tough times been able to increase its market share. While no one can predict the future, the last ten years have shown that Cisco has been a reasonably good asset to hold.

Why is that important? Because if you hold on to historically dominant companies like Cisco for a long period of time, they could become a relatively sizable asset in your portfolio—thanks to the splits—even if you do make periodic sales from time to time. And that, to me, is pretty strong evidence of the power of ownership.

Are you an owner in the same sense as the entrepreneur we talked about before? No. You don't run the business, and if you are like most people, you probably don't even vote on the direction of the company, although you receive proxies annually.

But the point is you could vote, and I think you should attend shareholder meetings. I would envision in the next 10 years we will probably have streaming video that will enable you to attend the meeting and probably file questions over the 'net via your PC. Democratization of capitalism is the trend, and so, too, I think is more active shareholders. Indeed, they could become a powerful lobbying influence. So I think ownership, even though it might be a minority ownership, is a critical concept for a Citizen Investor.

OWNERSHIP HAS ITS PRIVILEGES

There are other advantages of being a shareholder. You can call the investor relations department and ask questions so that you understand the company's business model a little better. That's a good place to go, in addition to your financial counselor, to learn what is going on.

Active ownership is important. Just because you don't own the whole company, the amount of shares you do own can become a very important asset to you over time and you always want to protect your assets. Yes, if things go wrong, your vote probably won't count a lot, but you can express your opinions and vote.

My sense is that most people are pretty inactive investors today. You're there, hopefully hitchhiking on the future growth of the company; and I think in a world where a news story can tempt you to get out of a stock, maybe at the wrong time, that is probably not the way to go. If you are an informed owner, you're probably less likely to make a decision to sell short term.

That raises an obvious question: Once you own a bulldog, do you ever sell?

The answer, of course, is yes—but the circumstances in which you sell—are extremely limited.

DO CITIZEN INVESTORS EVER SELL?

The first reason a Citizen Investor sells is when he or she recognizes he or she is wrong. You figured X would happen—there would be no major overhaul to the way health care is conducted in this country—and then Y happens—we adopt a socialized medical system, something like they have in Canada. You wake up. You realize the assumptions behind your decision to buy in the first place were faulty and so you get out.

The second reason to sell is you get extremely nervous about a competitive situation in the marketplace. A handful of promising companies are entering the field that your bulldog has traditionally dominated and you are not sure "your" company will be able to stave off the competition.

My sense is that it's probably a pretty good idea to make a partial sale when you sense there might be something bad going on. Sell off part of your position, and then if you were wrong—things were not as dire as you thought—you still have shares in the company.

This approach also applies to getting into a stock. It's not a bad idea to scale in over time. Rather than buying 1,000 shares at once, maybe two 500-share purchases make sense.

Now, implicit in everything that we have been talking about is that bulldogs are a long-term investment. If you are putting your kids through school in the near future—and by near term, I mean within the next two years—you probably shouldn't start investing heavily in bulldogs or any other kind of stock for that matter.

I think you might want to buy bulldogs for your kids when they are infants. But as we talked about before, the closer the time comes for paying for a goal, the more conservative you want to be with your investments. But with money that you are putting away for your retirement, a portion of your assets should be invested in great individual companies, maybe 13 to 20 of them spread over five sectors.

One final note on selling; everybody is risk-averse these days. But you don't hear about Warren Buffett trying to diversify heavily over a bunch of industries, and you don't often hear about him selling. It probably makes some sense from time to time, if you've got a big gain, to sell to rebalance your portfolio (i.e., put some of that gain into a new bulldog). If the company has gone from one-thirteenth or one-twentieth of your portfolio to being worth a quarter of it, it probably makes some sense to lighten up. But, as a rule, I'm not in favor of religiously rebalancing every quarter or even every year.

Now on diversification in general, my advice is the same as it was before. You want to shoot for owning between 13 and 20 stocks, probably in four or five sectors. So if it is five sectors, you've got around three or four stocks per sector to invest in.

It's a pretty good idea to spread it around. Try not to weight any one group too heavily. I made the mistake of over-weighting technology, and, like a lot of other people, it cost me money over the last couple of years.

If you are going to invest in five areas, technology should be one of the five, but that, by my definition, means it shouldn't be more than 20% of your portfolio.

And certainly don't go hog wild into one stock. Yes, you want to be an owner, but you don't need to own the whole company. And, as I said earlier, I'm not talking about putting all your money in bulldogs, although you want to feel extremely confident about the ones you own.

Still, you want to spread out your investments over several styles. For example, I personally own small-cap and large-cap value funds.

It makes a great deal of sense to be diversified, maybe weighting growth slightly more heavily than value since the growth style has been out of favor in recent times. A 60 percent growth stocks/40 percent value stocks split is what makes sense to me at this time. That isn't to diminish "value" bulldogs. It's just a suggestion that you have a more balanced approach than just growth.

You want to have both growth and value. If one group becomes dominant, you may want to reduce your holdings a bit, and add to the group that is out of favor, to try to take advantage of the inefficiencies in the market that give you more bang for your investment buck.

As a Citizen Investor, you are always trying to increase the value of your assets.

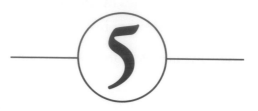

SEARCHING FOR BULLDOGS

Everyone's heard, "buy good companies and hold them." But a lot of people wonder if there is a way to shortcut the process?

The holding on part is relatively easy. Once you find a good firm, as long as it delivers operating performance, you don't sell.

But what about finding these firms in the first place? Can that be done quickly? If there is a shortcut, it stems from a lot of work. As a Citizen Investor, you need to learn how to find dominant companies, the bulldogs I've been talking about. Once you know what to look for, spotting them is relatively easy, but getting to that point can take a while.

But it's worth the commitment. In fact, there's a huge vested interest on my part, and on my firm's part, to deal with informed individuals. I think one of the greatest things we can do is to teach a person, via firsthand experience, what successful investing is all about.

A bulldog like Medtronic which has performed historically is a wonderful example.

Medtronic is a company that, as we have seen, has been delivering an average of 20% earnings growth over the last two decades or so. Up until the last two years, the stock has been a real winner, and history has shown that pullbacks have been temporary.

How does a Citizen Investor find companies like Medtronic?

Well, first you decide you are going to go looking for them. This is no small point. You need to be committed to all the things we have talked about before:

◆ **A disciplined approach to investing.** You have developed a strategy that involves owning dominant, winning companies and you are going to stay with it, regardless of what is going on in the overall markets at any given time.

◆ **The willingness to be patient.** You are going to stick with the strategy for as long as it takes. You've seen what

a patient approach has done for a great investor like
Warren Buffett.

◆ **The resolve to think like an owner.** Your focus is on
the long-term operating performance of the business
you are investing in and not the day-to day movement
of the stock price.

OK, you have decided to follow my Citizen Investor
strategy and you want to find bulldogs for part of your
portfolio. Where do you find them?

Well, it turns out that there are criteria you can use to
screen for them. Bulldogs—no matter where they are found—
have some things in common.

Let me give you the ten factors I look for, the things that
serve as my checklist before I invest in a company that I hope
turns out to be a bulldog.

A POTENTIAL-BULLDOG CHECKLIST

Here's a list of characteristics of companies that have
historically fit the bulldog criteria, along with some examples
of classic bulldogs who have, in prior times, exemplified each
of the traits. I'm not presenting it as a shopping list for you,
only as a look back at what has worked in the past.
Remember, a stock that has historically performed like a

bulldog has to continually prove its case to the market and its customers—a bulldog isn't a bulldog forever. And, again, this book is not intended to be a list of historical bulldogs for you to call your broker about. After reading the list below, it will be clear what to look for.

1. They sell a high-quality product or service. I can't think of a bulldog that offers customers even a mediocre product, or provides a service that you would describe as simply adequate. Bulldogs provide customers with, if not the best, then close to the best, product or service in the category they serve. I think of 3M whose culture has historically encouraged and rewarded innovation. Whether it's Post-It Notes, abrasives, coating, or medical products, the company has emphasized quality, and, for this discipline, it has won the Malcolm Baldridge National Quality Award.

2. They have a leadership position in the marketplace. One reason they have earned it is because of the culture within the company. Organizations that are bulldogs strongly believe that their customers deserve exceptional service and superior products. As a rule, these are very customer-driven, customer-focused companies. They work hard to understand what their customers want and, more often than not, they provide it year after year. Microsoft comes to mind immediately. The company established dominant market share in operating system software early on in the game and has continued to leverage that position in order to dominate other software applications.

3. They have superior management. Obviously, you can tell that by looking at the numbers, but I would suggest that you don't stop there. You want a company where they don't have a lot of people leaving, where turnover is substantially below the industry average. You want a culture of confidence where management is used to competing and winning. Hopefully, you can find firms that have had the same senior management in place for a while and a company where you can see that they spend a lot of time grooming the next generation of managers to replace the ones who are currently running the company. And you definitely want the CEO to have thought a lot about his or her successor.

In recent years, MBNA Corporation has epitomized this quality. The majority of senior executives have been with the company for over a decade; this management team has fueled earnings per share (EPS) growth at an average annual rate in excess of 20%. And knowing the importance of succession planning, MBNA has had a very effective employee development program.

4. They are supremely focused. These companies have a very defined business objective. With the best bulldogs, you can tell at a glance that they understand what business they are in and what they are trying to accomplish because they can easily explain that vision to you.

How can you discover if the company you are thinking of investing in has this kind of clarity? It is easy enough to find out, as we have seen. Read the letter from the chairperson or president in the annual report—it is invariably one of the very first things you see—or look at the way the company communicates with everyone. Winners are focused. Companies that are clear about what they want to do are equally clear about getting their message across. They will say: "These are our objectives and our strategy; here's how we want to employ our capital and assets." And they will also let you know what their profit and sales targets are.

Intel has been an example of a company that in the past has taken its annual report seriously, using that publication to reveal candid information about its objectives and business line outlook, and to critically evaluate past business decisions.

5. You want to look to an ongoing commitment to market dominance. One way to find that is to ask a series of questions:

- ◆ Does the company have a major commitment to research and development as a means of growing the business?
- ◆ Are they the low-cost producers?

◆ Have they figured out strategies and tactics that could give them a sustainable competitive advantage over established players in the field?

◆ Does it seem that they have a pretty good idea about how they would handle new competitors in their field?

In short, you are looking to see if they have a plan for staying on top in their market sector through a strategy of leadership and renewal.

Wal-Mart Stores has been a classic example of a company that has done this well. It built a very efficient distribution system and focused early expansion on small cities and large towns, where established, smaller stores couldn't compete on price and selection. More recently, the company took over the No. 1 spot for American grocers, leveraging higher margins from their traditional household goods business to undercut the prices offered by the traditional grocery chains.

6. Is there a record of growth and the probability of future growth? You want to investigate a company to see if it has a business model that can replicate itself without a huge leap in faith. In other words, you want to find companies that can continue to predictably do what they say they are going to do and will be able to do it fairly easily. Pharmaceutical companies are probably a great example of an industry that has set a pretty solid standard for growth.

Is there a kind of benchmark you should shoot for? Yes. I think you want to find corporations that are growing their earnings by at least 5% to 7% a year. The really outstanding companies tend to grow in excess of 10%.

If I find a company that has done that for a number of years—and that I feel reasonably confident will be able to continue to produce that kind of excellent performance in the years ahead—I am a buyer.

Look at Pfizer, Inc. From 1998 to 2003, the firm's pharmaceutical development program has been much more effective at producing drugs to offset patent expirations than their competitors. Consequently, it has had a compound annual growth rate for EPS of 15.9% during that last five-year period.

7. You want financial integrity... and that means a strong balance sheet, a company that is capable of financing its own growth, rather than borrowing. Traditionally you'd look for companies where debt is no more than 30% of total capitalization.

Coca Cola, in addition to keeping its customers loyal, has repeatedly achieved high returns on equity without the use of excessive debt. Coca Cola's debt-to-capitalization ratio is a mere 4.7% (based on June, 2002 balance sheet data and the close on Oct. 4, 2002), and its steady cash flows have served historically to sufficiently fund future growth activities.

What about companies like Enron and WorldCom where all the financial success has ended up in a pink cloud of lawsuits, accusations, and bankruptcy? Unfortunately, it's unlikely that an individual can determine if a company is fraudulent about its numbers. You can take solace in the fact that, with the recently enacted regulations that have come out of the corporate accounting scandals, anyone who does this faces serious jail time and are likely required to return ill-gained profits. Despite the headlines, integrity is still essential to a successful business career in our country.

8. You want to invest in world-class competitors. Is this company best of breed in the world? And, having said that, as markets move toward globalization, does their product line provide an element of scale that gives them a sustainable competitive advantage worldwide?

Nokia has fit this criterion in the past. Based on 2001 sales, Nokia was the market share leader for cell phone handsets in Europe, North America, and Asia. The company has tried to innovate its products based on market research, delivering what customers want even though that often differs from country to country.

9. There is demand for their products in good times and bad. You don't want to invest in feast-or-famine cyclical companies. By definition, there will be periods when a company that prospers in one part of an economic cycle and struggles in another will find it difficult to grow its sales and earnings. You're looking for companies that tend to have solid demand for their goods or service in even weak economies.

10. They are diversified. No, not in the sense that GE is diversified. GE is the traditional conglomerate that is in everything from financial services (GE Capital) to airplane engines to television. (It owns NBC.)

But it is diversified in the sense of Johnson & Johnson, which has had the whole line of medical products, from over-the-counter (Band-Aids and baby shampoo) to prescription drugs to medical devices. My sense is that the past track record becomes questionable if you have to bet the whole company on one new product that must get FDA approval. What you are looking for is a robust product line that is diversified throughout the category in which the company competes.

And that's the checklist. These are the major things that I look for in terms of criteria when I think of investing in a company I hope is a bulldog.

Your Bulldog Checklist:

Here are the criteria I use to try to find the next bulldog:

◆ They sell a high-quality product or service.

◆ They have a leadership position in the marketplace.

◆ They have superior management.

◆ They are supremely focused.

◆ I can see an ongoing commitment to market dominance.

◆ There is a record of growth and the probability of future growth.

◆ They have financial integrity.

◆ They are a world-class competitor.

◆ There is demand for their products in good times and bad.

◆ They are diversified.

CAN YOU SCREEN FOR THESE TYPES OF COMPANIES?

Sort of.

We run screens all the time for companies that have high returns on equity, high compound earnings growth, and high revenue growth; and often they are a great starting point, but the screens themselves are not enough.

What you are really looking for is a business that has been able to grow at above-average rates and deliver the financials it has promised and do both those things for an extended period of time. That means you have to get beyond the numbers and truly understand these kinds of firms.

Wouldn't it be great to own a business where all they do is continue to do what they have in the past, and along the way come up with better ways of doing it? For example, over time, they keep introducing new products, keeping their product line fresh.

That, to me, is what you're looking for—an evidenced ability to grow, coupled with a business model that's understandable enough to lead you to believe they can deliver superior financial results over the long term.

These are the types of firms you are looking for, and while the raw numbers can help you find them, you have to go further and do some research, potentially enlisting some people to help you find them.

One of the questions, of course, is whether your financial advisor at a full-service financial services firm can help you.

CAN YOUR BROKER BE A HELP?

It all looked so easy. When markets were defying gravity in the late '90s and early part of the new millennium, on-line trading looked like the newest form of home entertainment. From the comfort of your den, basement, or local coffee shop, you could buy and sell stocks for easy profits. Who needed financial consultants?

Three years and a combined drop of 6,000 Dow and Nasdaq points later, the go-it-alone strategy fell into the dustbin of hindsight. Reasoned, intelligent, professional financial advice has returned to its place as the most valuable commodity in the market today. Even if you accept the bulldog strategy of buying-and-holding dominant companies, it has become obvious that the advice of a financial pro is worth every penny it might cost you.

The true sign of a solid investment relationship is that the goal is to provide the client with wealth-building guidance. Our business is very much a relationship business, one that's built on trust over time. The final filter is that investor benefit drives all activity. So my guess is that if the financial professional isn't providing reasonable advice about good stocks, he or she is at a competitive disadvantage to those who understand the important role knowing what you own plays in individual stock investment.

More important, it's my sense that, given the kind of market we have been through over the last couple of years, clients will be demanding a more pronounced stock selection focus. A true hallmark of professionalism on the part of the broker will be the ability to structure effective and efficient portfolios.

And what that means is that the broker will want to act in the best interests of the client, not only because it is the right thing to do for the client, but also because clients will demand it.

And one way your broker can be of assistance is to help you become a patient investor.

I've found—and I think brokers have, too—that with good companies it's almost better to just hold them through the bad times rather than trying to lighten up or sell them on the way down (with the intention of buying them later when they start to climb). I don't know anybody smart enough to buy just before a stock goes back up. Once again, if we want proof of that we can look at the track record of the man who has been called "the world's greatest investor." Warren Buffett doesn't rebalance, he doesn't try to lower positions, he keeps good stocks for long periods, and that's one reason why he's so incredibly wealthy.

Digging a Little Deeper

Now that we have touched on the most important aspects of the book, let's go a little deeper.

One of the things investors have been told since the beginning of time is "past performance is no guarantee of future results." And that is absolutely correct. Just because a company turned in stellar numbers yesterday is no guarantee that it will continue to do so tomorrow. You don't have to look much further than today's headlines to see that is the case.

But when it comes to bulldogs, there is another adage that comes to mind. It is a line that Damon Runyon, the man who wrote the story that the musical *Guys and Dolls* is based on, was fond of uttering: "It may be that the race does not always go to the swift, nor the battle to the strong, but that is the way to bet."

And I think that is true when it comes to bulldogs. You want to start your search with companies that have demonstrated that they can grow their earnings at an above-average rate over a long period of time.

Traditionally, as I said, the average company can grow earnings at 5%, maybe 7% a year. There are very few companies that can do substantially better than that, even during the best of times. In the '80s, for example, there were only 143 companies out of the universe of the 6,000 largest publicly held firms that delivered at least 15% compounded earnings growth over the 10-year period.

So, searching for bulldogs is a challenge. And it is easier if you start with companies that have a track record of having done it.

There are not that many great companies for wealth creation. When you find one, keep it.

SPOTTING BULLDOGS EARLY

How about getting in early on a potential bulldog, one that is destined to turn in the numbers we have talked about, but hasn't done it yet.

Can you do it?

The only time I can even remember being present at the official birth of a bulldog was when Cisco went public. A lot of people felt as though the company was going to be a huge winner, and this time the crowd was right and it worked out that way.

But the Cisco IPO may be the exception that proves the rule because I'm reminded of any number of IPOs, especially during the Internet bubble, that were going to be "the next Cisco," that have never panned out.

I think remembering the ones that didn't work out is more instructive. One of the things to recognize about bulldog investing is that you want to be dealing with companies that have financial integrity. That means a quality balance sheet with no more than 30% of debt in most cases. It means they've got current earnings, and they are not betting the ranch on a new technology.

And if you are going to require those qualifications, then it is clear you are dealing with real businesses with current and sustainable financial credentials.

Yes, there are the rare, in-the-know institutional investors, who are in the position to own shares in a company before it is profitable and that eventually turns into a wonderful franchise. Everyone has a story about laser surgery firms or optical networking companies that hit it big when they went public and made the investing careers of some investors. But, I'm here to tell you that the winners are the extreme exception. As alluring as it is to swing for the fences on unproven stocks, the vast majority of firms without earnings don't turn into the dominant companies you are looking for. Taking the gamble isn't worth the risk. And managing risk and reward are what the Citizen Investor strategy is all about.

The point is that once a firm is profitable and earnings estimates are published, you have the opportunity to judge the desirability of a company based on its financial results. As a definitive track record unfolds, there will be plenty of opportunities to make the decision to buy them or avoid the risk. Assuming your risk acceptance profile is like mine, it's hard to make a case for owning companies that don't have earnings.

You want to focus on companies with strong current operating financials, financial integrity, and the stability a solid balance sheet provides. Any company that has had to make wholesale restatements of its earnings should be seriously questioned as a holding.

The single riskiest thing I think an investor can do is own companies that don't have current earnings. As an owner, or financial professional who recommends one of these companies, the only thing you can say when the stock goes down is "there are more sellers than buyers," and that excuse leaves me cold.

It is best to concentrate on established companies with a history of earnings.

OK, so companies right out of the gate are probably not going to help you. But is there a tip-off that a perfectly fine stock is going to turn into a bulldog?

The first step you should take is to find out how the company competes against its peers. Judged against them, does the stock look like an up-and-comer?

If it does, then it has to deliver—over time. Doing it once or twice doesn't cut it.

To qualify as a bulldog, the company must be consistent. And that means you want to be careful about a company that is soaring on the merits of one product. It may look like a bulldog initially, but when demand for its single product fades, it usually does not keep to that stellar form.

Much better than trying to be early—and being wrong the vast majority of the time—is recognizing that you are looking for companies that have proven themselves to be dependable. Buy them and focus on their *financial* performances. As long as they perform, keep them.

GOING DOWN ONE MORE LEVEL

We are almost there. But there is one more variation to discuss.

You've spotted established firms that show all the signs of being bulldogs, but they don't satisfy absolutely every element of the checklist. Does that eliminate them? Are some of the variables more important than others?

Is solid earnings growth more important than being global? Should you be willing to put up with debt that represents 50% of total capital, or is a dominant market share all that matters?

In other words, how do you weigh the variables?

First of all, you can't expect a company to have all ten criteria. I believe it all starts at the revenue line. That's the one figure companies can't engineer. I do look for operating leverage as a result of cost efficiencies and management effectiveness creating a business where a company might grow revenues at 15%, and earnings at 20% or so. In essence, they are spring-loaded because they are so productive.

But sales are sales and they are either growing dramatically or they are not. So that is the first place to look.

The second thing I would look for is earnings growth, higher revenues in the long term are more important than earnings, but you do need to see that those sales are scoring meaningful bottom-line growth.

Should you be willing to put up with a firm that has 50% of its total capital in debt? I don't like the 50% mark. I think anything above 30% gets to be kind of risky. I would be willing to consider a company with higher debt if part of its business plan is to lower the debt over a reasonable period of time to a level of 30% of total capital or less.

Market share leadership changes over time. So, it's critical to keep an eye on product movement and momentum. Sometimes, the best bulldog is a hungry bulldog, working hard to move up from a number three market position. That aside, it's probably best to stay with companies with the top one or two rank in their sector. Proven leadership is a very important element to look for.

What Do You Pay?

Armed with the checklist, you go searching for established bulldogs, and, lo and behold, you find one. What do you pay for it? Does price even matter if you are convinced you have found a firm that you think is a true winner?

It's wonderful if you can buy a bulldog at a P/E (price to earnings ratio) lower than its growth rate, based on forward estimates. So if the company has been trading at 12 times earnings, but it is expected to grow those earnings at 15% a year, you have a company worth a closer look.

Does the strategy, "buy on weakness", work for bulldogs?

Absolutely, it does. Market declines proved wonderful opportunities to acquire national treasure-type stocks at attractive prices. Sometimes stocks never trade at a P/E discount to their growth rates. But they do drop to levels that represent good values relative to their historic valuation ranges. The general rule is, as in life, you get what you pay for. If a stock trades on the cheap, there often is a good reason for it.

Remember, you are looking for extraordinary businesses, but it's not unusual for the market to misprice them. I don't know a mechanical way of screening for that, other than to be diligent and monitor the price of bulldogs closely.

I think it's going to be tough in today's world to find a corporation that has grown earnings 18% to 20% a year, that trades at 13 times forward earnings. But if you can find one—and MBNA was in that area in June, 2003—then it is a pretty good deal.

Markets do swing to extremes and unusual circumstances can cause the stock market to mark great businesses down to fire-sale valuations. For instance, recently, a few banks with problem loans to financially compromised telecom companies, took down the whole group.

I think that in today's market, two times the growth rate is a fair price to pay for a company you think will become a bulldog.

In today's world, established companies normally trade at two times their growth rate, and that seems to hold true even when we have a depressed stock market. That, to me, would seem to be the going rate for one of these stellar stocks.

But what you're really looking for is a company that can replicate very high earnings growth rates over long periods of time, and so I don't pay overriding attention to what the company is currently trading for. I try to not let the trading calls—"XYZ Co. at $18 is a buy!"—that seem to make up a lot of Wall Street research, affect me. You don't want to get too mechanical when it comes to P/E. The reason? You're acting as a Citizen Investor, not a renter of your company's stock certificate, and you believe the company has a very compelling business opportunity at a price that will only appreciate with the passing of years.

This reminds me of Cisco, the example cited earlier, where $10,000 became $12 million. But there were three times in a five-year period where the stock fell 50%, and you could have bought it relatively cheaply. When it comes to bulldogs, I tend not to focus solely on the price of the stock. I concentrate on the financials, how the company is doing now, and whether its current results are sustainable.

WHEN DO YOU SELL?

Everything we just talked about is true, but it does not negate an obvious—and sad—fact of life. Once you own a bulldog, there will be periods of market declines. The great companies of the world did not achieve their remarkable gains in a straight line that always headed higher. There were periods of decline along the way.

Sometimes these companies get caught in a general sell-off. It seemed during the first half of 2002, for example, the only thing that all stocks did was move constantly lower—and sometimes stocks get caught up by events in the media and are hammered down in price by news and rumors.

The question is, once a Citizen Investor owns a great company, if it goes down, what do you do?

Buy more?

You probably shouldn't.

I've always felt that rather than buying more, or averaging down, it makes sense to add a new position. If you own dominant companies, odds are you have a relatively concentrated portfolio. And there's always a chance that you're wrong. So why should you consider lowering the risk by adding another bulldog to your portfolio? I'm not a big believer in doubling down, or increasing holding in a stock.

Lowering risk in a portfolio of quality companies is simple: add a new great company.

Now, what do you do with your existing positions in light of a declining market? I make this mistake all the time. When Cisco was trading at a market capitalization in excess of 10 times its annual sales and a P/E multiple that was three to four times its growth rate, I didn't sell. If I had sold it at $80 I probably would have been buying it back at $70, $60, $40 and just had less of a loss. These good companies tend not to go away.

When you are looking at a price-to-earnings ratio that is three to four times the company's growth rate, or a multiple of 10 times sales, it is probably a pretty good time to lighten up your position.

But that brings us to an important point. Suppose your bulldog is going the other way, and the numbers have started to decline. Then what? In other words, when is a bulldog not a bulldog?

ARE BULLDOGS ALLOWED TO SLIP?

Must sales, earnings, and growth steadily increase?

Is a bulldog allowed to miss a quarter, a year?

The answer is, the more a company disappoints, the less it is a bulldog. There are extenuating circumstances, of course. For example, as the entire economy slows to a crawl—or worse—it is not realistic to expect sales and earnings growth of 20% a year indefinitely out of any company, no matter how wonderful its pedigree.

So, yes, these companies can miss a quarter or years of quarters like Cisco, Intel, and others and still be a dominant company. It makes sense when a stock gets ridiculously overvalued, to take some money off the table and not remain totally dogmatic, convinced that you have to hold on to the bulldog until the end of time.

BUY AND HOLD STILL WORKS

Buy and hold is under a lot of scrutiny right now. It's hard to find a monthly financial publication that doesn't take a swipe at it, saying that it doesn't work anymore. The market, they say, has become too volatile.

And yet two of the most successful investors on the planet—Peter Lynch and Warren Buffett—are pretty much long-term buy-and-hold people, and they have done pretty well.

We've got a pretty strong historical sampling that shows that over time there are very few companies that can grow at 15% a year. If you can find one that can grow at 10% or more for a reasonably long period of time, you have a bulldog, and I would buy it and hold on.

PATIENCE

When I'm talking to groups on behalf of RBC Dain, I like to use a story about the painter Vincent Van Gogh to make a point about patience and the power of time.

My story goes like this:

By all accounts, Vincent Van Gogh, the best-known impressionist painter of the 19th century, sold only one painting in his life, *Red Vineyard at Arles,* for the equivalent of $100 in 1890.

Assuming that's true, we can guess that any other paintings he did would have sold for about the same amount, about $100, if he were "lucky" enough to find a buyer during his lifetime.

One of his greatest paintings, *Sunflowers*, was never sold when he was alive, but it was auctioned off nearly 100 years later for $39.9 million.

People in the audience smile and shake their heads at how much the value of that painting appreciated, when they hear me tell them that. Invariably, their reaction is to what it would have sold for under our hypothetical scenario— $100—and what it eventually went for, nearly $40 million.

But to me, the story makes a different point, a point about the wonders of time and compounding interest.

Here's what I mean: the S&P 500 total return (price plus dividends) averaged 13% from the end of World War II through the end of 1999.

Any guess at the compound rate $100 (our presumed price of Van Gogh's *Sunflowers*) has to appreciate at to reach $39 million over 100 years?

Amazingly, the answer is an average annual return of 13.7%.

If your parents invested $100 on the day you were born and the stock they chose matched that 13.7% return, you'd celebrate your 100th birthday with $39.4 million in the bank, the same amount of money you would have gotten if your ancestors were lucky enough to have bought a Van Gogh and passed it down through the years.

The *Sunflowers* story is a great hypothetical that demonstrates the point implicit in the Citizen Investor investment strategy, or any investment strategy for that matter, that you have to be patient.

To exaggerate to make the point: You need to understand that the stock you just bought is not going to double during the 20 minutes you are watching its ticker symbol flash by on CNBC, CNNfn or Bloomberg.

Nobody likes to be patient. But there are profound reasons why all of us should value the aspect of time when it comes to investing.

Experts who are conversant with risk and risk management view time as perhaps the single most important factor in any investment program. They see it as the lever that helps us extract the highest possible investment returns.

There are a couple of reasons I think people should be patient. Let's go through them now.

Everyone Needs to Think Long Term

The actuaries say that today when people stop work at age 65 they are probably going to be retired for 18 years. That's how much our life expectancies have expanded.

So, the first thing that 18 years in retirement tells us is if we are investing for the long term, there is no rush. The long term will actually be the very long term.

Now, implicit in this is that most of us are probably going to be investors even after we retire. Very few people retire at age 65 already having a lump sum that will fund an 18-year retirement. We are going to need to keep our money growing, even once we stop working.

That is one reason to be thinking long term. If you would like to be a Citizen Investor, you should plan on owning stocks for all of your life.

A portfolio made up of all bonds and cash probably won't generate enough income for you, and if you go with all cash, or cash equivalents like certificates of deposit or money market funds, you could actually lose ground. Let's take a quick step back to show why that is the case.

Historically, cash has returned 3.8% a year, while inflation has averaged 3.1%. That means your "real" rate of return on cash—what you earn after inflation is taken into account—is just 0.7% a year. (That is the 3.8% nominal rate of return minus the 3.1% inflation rate.)

And that is before you pay taxes on the 3.7% you earned. (Unfortunately, you are taxed on that full 3.7%, not the 0.6% real return.)

When you factor in taxes, your real rate of return on a cash investment could very well be negative. For example, if you are in the 28% tax bracket—a substantial possibility for people planning on drawing down their investments in retirement—your real rate of return would be -0.4% once taxes are accounted for. You actually lose money!

Stocks, Bonds, Bills, and Inflation 1925–2002

Wealth indices of investments in the U.S. capital markets*

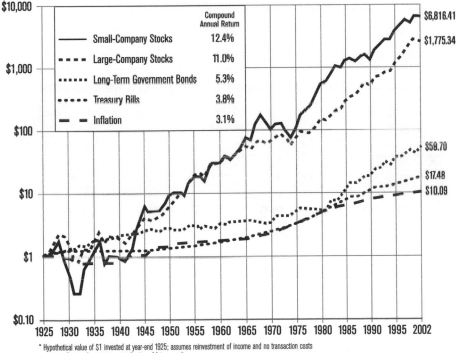

	Compound Annual Return
—— Small-Company Stocks	12.4%
■ ■ ■ ■ Large-Company Stocks	11.0%
••••••• Long-Term Government Bonds	5.3%
••••• Treasury Bills	3.8%
— — Inflation	3.1%

$6,816.41
$1,775.34
$59.70
$17.48
$10.09

* Hypothetical value of $1 invested at year-end 1925; assumes reinvestment of income and no transaction costs or taxes. Past performance is no indication of future results..

Source: Stocks, Bonds, Bills and Inflation® 2003 Yearbook, ©2001 Ibboson Associates, Inc.
Based on copyrighted works by Ibbotson and Sinquefield. All rights reserved. Used with permission.

That's not hyperbole. It's fact. Let's do the math.

Let's say you have $100,000 to invest and you put it in a cash equivalent, such as a money market fund or CD. Historically, cash equivalents have returned 3.7% a year. So, at the end of the year, you would have $3,700 in interest. Not great, but you would be ahead of the game, right?

Well, not quite. Remember, we haven't accounted for inflation or taxes. Using the 28% tax bracket figure we assumed above, you'd be left with $2,664, of that $3,700, in interest, making the return on your investment 2.66%. (And, of course, if you are subject to state or local income taxes, that number will be even less.)

But that 2.66% is before inflation is taken into account. Inflation typically averages 3.1%, so that reduces your "real return" to **a negative** 0.44%.

If you keep much of the money you are investing in cash or a cash equivalent, you may actually lose ground, once taxes and inflation are taken into account.

In other words, the $100,000 you had in year one, only has the buying power of $99,560 in year two. You have actually lost buying power! Check today's money market rates that are actually less than the rate of inflation. That means "cash equivalents" are a very safe, dependable way to lose money!

And in case you are wondering, if you find yourself in the 15% tax bracket in retirement, you'd basically break even. (You end up keeping $35 in interest after federal taxes. And, again, we haven't taken state or local taxes into account, so odds are you, too, would have a negative return.)

So given all this, maybe we ought to pay more attention to risk management tools, and one of the great risk management tools is time.

Here's why. If you look at the returns of the S&P throughout history, you will notice the shorter the time frame, the more volatile the returns. For example, in the best one-year period you would have made 52% on your money, and in the worst you lost 26%.

If that is all the information you had, you'd conclude that the odds of making money in the stock market, if you have a one-year time horizon, are about 50/50.

That leads me to say that if your time horizon is a year or less, you're really not investing, you're in the entertainment business; you're gambling.

However, if you had a five-year time horizon—and you could pick any five-year period you want—the range narrows substantially. In the best five-year period, you gained 23.9%

on your money and in the worst, you lost 2.4%. And, in fact, in this study there was only one five-year period where you lost money—that was in the one that ended December 31, 1974.

If you look at any 10-year period, the spread between highs and lows becomes even closer—and you would never have lost money. In the best 10-year period you made 19.3%, in the worst, 1.2%.

Rolling-Period Returns
S&P 500 Index: December 31, 1950–December 31, 2002

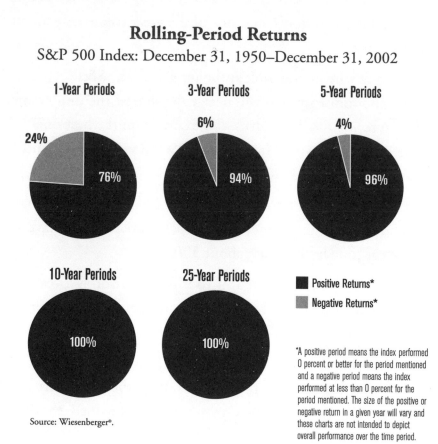

Source: Wiesenberger®.

*A positive period means the index performed 0 percent or better for the period mentioned and a negative period means the index performed at less than 0 percent for the period mentioned. The size of the positive or negative return in a given year will vary and these charts are not intended to depict overall performance over the time period.

So just buying an S&P index fund and owning it for long periods of time can be an effective way to make money, and the thing that keeps you in the game is the appreciation that comes from holding on to the fund over time.

There's another point to be made about this.

No matter how you look at the rates of return, most people conclude the market has delivered 10% a year on average over long periods. Indeed, it has been that way going back to 1926, a period that not only factors in the crashes of 1929 and 1987, but includes the dismal performance of the markets during the first part of this century as well.

Now, arguably, the best investors in stocks, Peter Lynch and Warren Buffett, compiled incredible returns in their tenures. In the 13 years when Lynch was manager of Fidelity's Magellan Fund, a $1,000 investment would have resulted in $28,000—nearly a 30% average annual return. In 38 years managing Berkshire Hathaway, Buffett returned shareholders a 22.2% compound average annual return. If anybody has ever done any better, I'd like to hear about it.

But it's important to look inside both investment disciplines that these men used.

While Buffett took a value approach, and Lynch looked for growth, both were investors. Neither bought tips; neither tried to time the market. Both bought companies with the idea of holding them for three to five years at the very least.

My sense is that for most of us, even though the "experts" today are saying "buy and hold is dead," the most important attribute in investing is to have patience.

Now, patience in and of itself is fine. You simply could buy an index fund and hold on. However, in declining markets, such as the one we experienced at the beginning of this decade, that means you are going to hold on as the overall value of your portfolio keeps steadily declining. If the market falls 20%, your index fund is going to fall 20% as well. That argues for two things:

◆ having something other than index funds
  in your portfolio; and

◆ being patient enough to let your investment
  strategy work.

I think the main cause of not being patient is the lack of having a discipline. You end up being all over the place. I would argue that most of us should include growth and value bulldogs in our portfolios at all times so we are positioned to take advantage of both.

Unless you think the market is ridiculously overvalued, you always want to have positions in stocks because, as we have seen, the long term trend has been that they will move higher along with the rest of the market. And even when the market is overvalued, I wouldn't get out completely. I would just lighten up my position and still have a certain amount of assets exposed to the market. Otherwise, you find yourself in a position of being a market timer and that isn't good for a number of reasons that we have talked about before.

To Review Why Market Timing Doesn't Work:

1. No one has proven to be smart enough to know exactly when the market will rise again after a decline. Opportunity costs are critical. If you miss those concentrated times when a stock goes back up, or the market goes back up, it can really hurt your total return.

2. The transaction costs of selling to get out and buying again to get back in, can reduce your returns by 1% to 2% on average.

3. Taxes on a short-term basis—that is, if you hold your investment for less than a year—can eat up most of the advantage of trying to own these stocks in the first place. Taxes are another hidden advantage that accrues to a long-term investor.

So, what I am saying is once you have an investment strategy, stay committed to it—which is another way of saying "being patient" is critical. If you are not, you could miss big moves, and you will certainly pay more in taxes and transaction costs than you need to.

But if you are patient? You will probably end up with a better rate of return.

Staying committed over the long haul makes sense. Odds are if you take this approach, over time, you are going to do quite well.

If You Are Not Patient, Something May Be Wrong

Given all the advantages of being patient, if you keep making moves—or are continuously itchy to make moves—it may be a tip-off that something is wrong.

If you are frequently trading bulldogs—or stocks that you hope will become bulldogs—it could be a sign that you're not confident in your investment strategy. If that is the case, then you're probably acting on emotion. You're not acting out of conviction, and my guess is you are suffering a huge cost as a result.

In the midst of the bear market of 1973-1974, a lot of people made the decision to shift everything out of stocks and into bonds, and they really hurt their portfolios—especially their retirement portfolios—long term.

I think we have to be really careful to avoid making bad decisions that will take us out of the asset class that has traditionally gone up 74% of the time and provided powerful, positive returns. So there are lots of reasons, particularly within the framework of a retirement plan, to be patient.

Some people just can't be patient. And while I'm not quite sure I understand why that is the case, I do understand for some people it is.

So, for them, what I'd recommend is still adopting a Citizen Investor strategy, but I would tell them (or you, if the impatient shoe fits) to concentrate on trying to buy bulldogs near their lows and selling partial positions when appropriate.

As I said, I think the buy-and-hold approach is simpler (there is less trading) and probably more effective long term (you don't have to worry about trying to time the market, and the tax rate on your gains will be less). But, if your temperament won't allow you to do it, here's how the alternative approach could work.

It would start the same way. You'd buy 13 to 20 bulldogs. You'd still be diversifying by industry—you'd want technology, retail, defense stocks, etc.—and by style; i.e. you'd have both growth and income.

Here, though, you would be purchasing those firms when they are relatively cheap and, in essence, you'd be looking to trade them. You'd sell when they became overvalued on the fundamentals. I don't think it would make sense to sell your entire position because these are firms that, by definition, are supposed to do very well over time. Still, if you are the impatient sort, you could sell part of your position as the stock rises and take some money off the table.

Does taking this approach—trading as opposed to buying and holding—make you a bad person? No. But it's probably not the best way to increase your overall return, for the reasons we talked about before.

Still, if you are someone who can't wait, let me give you another variation on what you could do.

You could take a fixed portion of your portfolio—say 10% or so—and devote it to fliers and the like. That way, you would still have most of your assets devoted to buying and holding good stocks, but you'd have enough money set aside to indulge your need for immediate gratification.

I think entertaining yourself this way is fine. If you go this route, I'd do it in a taxable account, rather than a retirement one, because you have so many benefits that will accrue to your advantage in retirement accounts by being patient—compounding and tax-deferral being the biggest two—so trading through it doesn't make a lot of sense.

Again, you can trade to any extent you want. But let me just point out that a good friend of mine, who is a manager of a big branch of a major brokerage firm, keeps track of how well his brokers do trading in their own individual option accounts. He has kept this record for years, and he tells me that although they may win occasionally, over the long term they all give it all back. He tells me there has not been one successful broker trading options for his own account—and these are all people who spend every working day participating in the stock market.

I think trading in general has proven to be more a loser's game than any other. But if you have an urge for excitement, from day trading, IPOs—whatever it involves—you make the decision. It's your money.

But recognize that it's a very tiny minority of people that have a facility for actually trading stocks successfully, and then if you decide to get into day trading or IPOs, or other aggressive strategies, I'd do it with a very small portion of your money.

How Patient Is Patient?

Convinced that you have to be patient—or at least patient with the bulk of your money—the next question is: How long do you need to wait?

I think a very patient investor in today's world would be someone who would be willing to wait for 18 months for fundamental proof that his or her investment thesis was correct, and be willing to live with that time frame until the market reflected the truth one way or another.

The reality is that I think that the marketplace today is requesting that brokerage firms give advice that is on the mark for the next six months. My sense is that, given the hideous market we have been in between 2000 and 2003, a lot of people believe buy and hold is dead. (I don't, but a lot of people do.) As a result, we are going to see a much more focused, transactional kind of investment advice, at least from most of the firms. And my sense is that it's going to be very difficult to produce the kind of returns that the markets have traditionally provided by offering that kind of short-term advice.

Besides, how much can short-term gains actually help you? How much does a 20% gain in one stock help, after (short-term) taxes and transaction fees are deducted? Once they are taken out, there is not as much left over as you might think.

*While you may feel good about catching a short-term move
in a stock's price, you might find that transaction expenses
and taxes eat up your return pretty dramatically.*

And, of course, when you are making short-term decisions
like this, and making them constantly, the opportunity to be
wrong is quite high.

I've got to tell you, though, that in the big decline we lived
through in 2001-2002, I have learned some things and have
amended my thinking a bit. I used to buy bulldogs and hold
them right down to the bottom because I wanted to stay
positive.

Going forward, if I ever had holdings like some of the
technology stocks which were trading at absurdly high
multiples as much as 15 times sales, three times growth rate
and 105 times earnings—I would act differently. Given those
kinds of valuation, I would make partial sales, probably selling
off a third of my holdings. That is the course I am going to
follow in the future. Even though the stock might be a
bulldog, I'm going to lighten up and trade around positions.
So, while my overall strategy will remain constant, I am
planning on tweaking it a little.

Even so, a lot of people question my intelligence for
sticking with a long-term strategy, and that reaction is one of
the things you have to live with.

But I have faith, and if you look at the returns historically—and it doesn't matter if you are a bull or bear—betting on the bull market makes more sense. The long-term trend is up.

Now, to the people who think I am deluding myself about future trends in the market, I will concede that my brand of investing does require hope. You have to believe that the market will continue to perform the way it has historically, going up the majority of the time and providing annualized returns somewhere around 10%.

What those numbers really mean is the market, in fact, does reward people for being patient and owning companies for a long period of time.

What Do You Do While You Are Waiting?

When I explain to people why they need to be patient, some people don't get it. Most of them do, but even those who accept the idea have some practical questions:

1. "How often do I check my portfolio if I have decided to be patient?"

2. "Can I use technical analysis to help me figure out which stocks I want to be patient with?"

3. "How long do I wait before I can reasonably conclude that I don't have a bulldog on my hands, just a dog?"

Let's take them one at a time, starting with how often you should check your portfolio.

I get my statement monthly, and I think that's often enough to look at the performance of the stocks you own. If you focus on the value of your stocks daily, unless you're really an easygoing individual, you can drive yourself crazy. (In down markets, even I tend to look at my statements only occasionally. It's too depressing.)

I think you also want to read the annual reports from each of the companies that you own and familiarize yourself with the benchmarks that management sets with regard to:

♦ revenues and earnings growth,

♦ any return on equity data or balance sheet targets, and

♦ new products in the pipeline.

And then, as we've said, you want to own companies that do what they say they are going to do. You want to hold management accountable.

WHAT ARE YOU WAITING FOR?

Now we've talked about being patient. But what is your payoff? What kind of reward are you hoping to get for waiting?

Well, at the very least, you want to do as well as the market has done traditionally. So, that would put you at a 10% annualized return.

Should you expect more? Sure. Within reason.

I think you begin by recognizing that Peter Lynch and Warren Buffett have done substantially better than the historical average, but even those investing superstars have reached limits on returns.

To me that then becomes the top level: 20%, with the 10% historical annualized return being the floor of what you are trying to achieve. Given those parameters, a return in the mid-teens would be wonderful. That would allow you to create wealth over time. For example, at 13% a year compounded, your money doubles in less than six years.

I try to buy stocks that will double over a three- to five-year time horizon. Sometimes it happens quicker, sometimes it doesn't, but I like to see earnings have the ability to double over a five-year time horizon, which equates to a 15% kind of compound earnings growth rate. That may or may not be realistic, but when it happens, it makes me happy.

GETTING PROFESSIONAL HELP

Now, you don't have to do this yourself. You could hire a professional money manager and give him or her marching orders to find you bulldogs you can buy and hold. There are a number of money managers who believe there are not that many great companies out there and that you should have core positions in the few established top performers and hold those core positions for long periods of time. In other words, these are money managers who specialize in investing in bulldogs.

Sure, there are a number of money managers who are looking for the short-term hit. But once you find a good money manager who believes as you do, stick with them. A good manager who doesn't change his or her strategy to match the latest fad, one who delivers compensatory returns over the long period, is a rarity today. Once you find one, keep them. And, by all means, give them the benefit of time to perform their risk-managed ability to deliver a return.

That brings us to question two.

Sometimes people ask me if I use technical analysis to discover bulldogs worth holding on to.

The answer is I do. I rely on my colleague Bob Dickey, our chief technical analyst at RBC Dain Rauscher, his charts and his technical work. And if he points out that one of my bulldogs is weak technically, we really look at it long and hard. That would not be the prime reason why we would sell it. The main reason to get out of the stock would be if we saw deterioration in the core business of the company, but the technicals are certainly a consideration.

But I think technicals absolutely are valid, and they are something to pay attention to, not just in bear markets, but in bull markets as well.

The thesis of this book is that there are very few good companies, and once you find one, it's a good idea to keep it unless you believe the business case is changing. Technical analysis may give you a clue that the business case is changing in a material way and it is time to get out.

If there's any flaw in technical analysis it's that it tends to treat all stocks as if they are commodities. My view, as you know, is that there are differences among stocks and that there are, indeed, a few rare companies that warrant being owned by individuals for the long term. These companies, these bulldogs, are the most likely to deliver performance for the long term.

But technical analysis could help me find out when I'm wrong about a stock. And if it does that, it is a big help. So I pay attention to technical analysis and use it, but it's not my prime motivation.

SPEAKING OF SELLING

And that brings us to question three: "How long do I wait before I can reasonably conclude that I don't have a bulldog on my hands, just a dog?"

This question is the most frequently asked question I get about patience. Boiled down, it's another way of asking why you would want to hold stocks on the way down.

The answer, and I don't mean to be flippant, is because I'm not smart enough to buy them back just before they go up.

Nobody, and I mean nobody, who is long in the market likes it when a stock they own is falling. It's painful to watch the share price decline. But, Peter Lynch said his greatest mistakes were selling good companies too soon. The mistake wasn't buying a company like Enron or WorldCom, but selling great companies long before he should have.

We live in a world that is focused on 20/20 hindsight. No one likes to be wrong, but we seem obsessed with trying to figure out what went wrong. And so when one of our bulldogs starts to fall, we hate it. It seems to be a (daily) reminder that we were wrong about picking that stock.

But you do have to be patient. Great stocks don't keep going up in a straight line.

Is This Time Different?

During the long, awful bear market that started in 2000, we all started to hear a new theme: The days of the market moving perpetually higher over time are gone forever.

Is this time different? Are the days of 10% annualized growth a thing of the past?

There is no way of answering that. No one knows for sure.

But, I do know this. "This time it's different," is always a dangerous argument. I heard it in 1973–1974 when we were mired in a horrific bear market, the Dow was in the three digits, and people said we'd never crack 1,000; and I heard again from the other side in the late '90s, when people said, "This time it is different, and the fundamentals no longer apply to investing." I'm even hearing it today.

I say, "This time it's the same."

And the reason I say that is because the economy has always recovered. There have always been corporate catastrophes; there have always been senior executives who were crooks. This time it seems like they have gotten a little colder hearted with WorldCom and Enron back to back, but we shouldn't forget PennSquareBank or the energy stocks in the '80s or Intercontinental Life Insurance in the '70s or any of the other earlier scandals.

I think the market presents a pretty convincing case that it goes up over time.

Historically, the returns have been powerful and positive, and if you have a three- to five-year time horizon, this long-term approach has worked well when it comes to returns.

And I think that will remain true in the next few years as well.

There are a number of reasons I say that.

First of all there's productivity. We're the most productive country in the world. If you look at Europe, their wages are rising quicker than their productivity. That is a sure sign of the competitive advantage our economy delivers.

We're the most innovative country in the world, with leadership positions in pharmaceuticals, software, hardware, entertainment, aerospace engineering, and biotechnology. These are things human beings want and need and buy and use up and then buy again and again. Given this, my sense is that this is not a time to sell everything and abandon your strategy.

Yes, the news recently has been horrific with regard to terrorism, and yes, the markets have been awful since just about the beginning of the century, and yes again, the economic data has been less than stellar.

But even given all that, I think the reality is that things are actually pretty good, despite what you see when you pick up a newspaper or you turn on a television. The economy will recover. The market will recover, and on average over time I expect the market will deliver about a 10% return.

For most of us that means that we should probably remain patient and expectant with the serious money in our retirement plans and maintain our commitments to stocks in the long term.

Besides, what is your alternative? Market timing? That simply doesn't work. Market timing is the belief that there is a guru, a psychic, or maybe a black box or computer program that can keep you out of the market when it is going down and get you back in just before it starts to go up.

That's virtually impossible.

There are two reasons I say that:

First, an investor who shifts from stock to cash will, by definition, miss out on some of the market's major moves higher.

There is a University of Michigan study that also proves the point. They looked at the market period of 1982–1987, covering the 1,276 trading days that ended August 25, 1987.

If you were in for the full 1,276 days, you made 26.3% on your money, but if you missed the 10 biggest days, your return would have been 18.3%. If you missed the 20 biggest days, it would have been 13.1%; missed the 30 biggest days, and you made 8.5%, and if you missed the 40 biggest days, you made just 4.3% on your money.

People who stayed completely in cash did better than the folks who missed the 40 biggest days. They earned 7.9% over that time. We should be careful about trying to time an asset that goes up most of the time.

The second reason that argues against market timing? The transaction costs of making the switches.

Being patient is hard. But when you look at the numbers, there really is no other alternative if you want to make money.

Remember Van Gogh.

REALISTIC
EXPECTATIONS

"**E**nough already," I hear you cry. "Let's get to the good stuff. How much can I make as a Citizen Investor? What kind of returns can I expect?"

Well, with the traditional caveat that there are never any guarantees on Wall Street, history shows that, over time, a portfolio that follows the principles we have talked about so far has been averaging 10% a year.

Now, we have to take a step back to put that number into perspective.

With that historic return in mind, what I am suggesting is that a long-term strategy based on investing in bulldog companies gives you the possibility to do better.

Two reasons.

First, you'll own superior businesses, and that will put you in good company. While I can't prove it, my sense is that a number of premium money managers—the folks who have proven themselves to be the best—recognize the long-term value of investing in superior businesses.

These premium money managers understand and gravitate toward companies that deliver superior financial results, and the really good ones don't trade in and out of these stocks.

The second reason: scarcity. Historically, there are very few companies that, in my opinion, deliver above-average earnings for extended periods of time. When they see a company that has earnings that are predictable, dependable, and repetitive over time, they become confident in the company's ability to deliver those results.

As the quarterly reports provide tangible proof of a company's premium business credentials and show that the firm keeps making the numbers, investors realize this is a business they would like to own. They don't tend to think about selling it. It's easy for them to envision it doing quite well, even during market swoons, because they know the demand for its products will be there. And so they, too, hold on—perhaps even buying more shares on the dips.

Confidence and quality financial performance add up to deliver a strong combination that owners dream about.

Given this, I think expectations should be higher for a Citizen Investor portfolio than for something like an index fund that mirrors the performance of the S&P 500.

BUT WE ARE ONLY TALKING A LITTLE BIT MORE, RIGHT?

Take a look at the chart below. It shows how a little extra over the average can result in strong returns.

A Little Difference Can Mean a Lot						
$10,000 invested for this many years	4% annual return	6% annual return	8% annual return	10% annual return	12% annual return	14% annual return
1	10,400	10,600	10,800	11,000	11,200	11,400
5	12,166	13,382	14,693	16,105	17,623	19,254
10	14,802	17,908	21,589	25,932	31,058	37,072
15	18,009	23,965	31,721	41,772	54,735	71,379
20	21,911	32,072	46,609	67,275	96,462	137,434
25	26,658	42,918	68,484	108,347	170,000	264,619
30	32,433	57,434	100,626	174,454	299,599	509,501

*This chart presents a hypothetical scenario for illustrative purposes only. Returns depicted do not take into account fees, commissions, or other expenses associated with investments.

So there's a pretty compelling reason to try to get an extra 2% increase over the average. To get that extra 2%—and hopefully more—you want to find a discipline that you can have confidence in. And, to me, a Citizen Investor portfolio of bulldogs is such a discipline. It gives me confidence because I can envision these businesses enduring and delivering strong financial performances for years. Of course, there are no guarantees that any stock strategy will deliver these types of returns.

BULLDOGS IN GOOD TIMES AND BAD

Now let me stress what you already know. Even if you have the perfect strategy, you won't receive a 10% or a 12% return every year. There will be years where even the best companies will watch their shares go down in value. If we have selected superior companies, should our performance longer term offset any bear market dilution?

I'm reminded of Warren Buffett's portfolio of investments, which are basically represented by Berkshire Hathaway stock itself. At its peak in 1998, the company was trading at $84,000 a share. Two years later, in March of 2000, it got down to $40,800. Which means Berkshire Hathaway has declined over 50% more than the worst bear market since the Depression.

As I write, the stock is somewhere in the $70,000 level, but it's not back to where it was at the top.

The point here is that sometimes investing can be painful. But over the long pull there is promising opportunity, and, as I have been saying over and over, it's almost impossible to time your way out of the market before things get bad, and then get back in on an attractive basis when things are good.

As a fundamentally driven investor, you can take comfort in the fact that if a company is hitting its numbers and sequentially increasing its earnings, it will eventually be reflected in the price of the stock.

Are people guilty of irrational exuberance when times are good for bulldogs? Absolutely. Stocks—including bulldogs—can get bid up to unrealistic levels—two, three, and even four times their growth rate. And as I said before, when that happens, it makes sense to make a partial sale to take some money off the table.

When would you follow this strategy? For me, it would be when a stock begins to trade at a P/E ratio that is two-and-a-half to three times its growth rate. At that point, it is substantially overvalued.

You normally don't see that in value stocks, but in growth stocks you can see a company getting bid up to wild levels.

And when that happens, you should sell a portion of your position in that particular bulldog. Then you have the choice of investing in something else—another bulldog—or holding on to your money until the stock comes back down to earth.

Why only a partial sale? Because, as we discussed before, most of us are just not nimble enough to go all the way out of a great name and come back in at a more attractive price. We tend to get out and never get back in for the eventual ride higher that those earnings will drive.

So, that is how I would handle the good times—sell a bit when things get nutty, and hold on to the rest of your position.

As for the bad times? Well, when times are bad, bulldogs can get killed. You have irrational despair. Look at Automatic Data Processing.

ADP just missed their quarterly numbers in June, 2002, and the stock got completely hammered in the marketplace. Its shares fell more than 22% the day after it warned of slower profit growth. ADP's stock was off more than $9, which means the company lost $6 billion in market value that day, and that kind of reaction didn't make any sense. That was the cheapest valuation for ADP versus fundamental measures since 1991.

Home Depot was hit about the same time. It got down to 16.5 forward (the next 12 months) earnings. At that level, the stock traded at the lowest valuation-to-book ratio it has had since going public.

One of our brokers called recently and said, "I've been waiting 10 years for a chance to buy ADP, and I'm going to do it today." And I think that was the right approach to take.

So, from time to time we do get to be beneficiaries of irrational despair. The question is after we have a period where all stocks seem to do is fall in value every day—a situation we had in 2000–2002—do people have the stomach to buy anything? But it is exactly at those moments that these stocks represent a great deal of value.

BULLDOGS VERSUS THE MARKET

When you add up everything we have talked about so far, the conclusion seems pretty clear. Over the long term, companies that deliver dependably superior financial results normally outperform the market as a whole.

You should expect bulldogs to outperform the market.

But as we have seen, they won't turn in that kind of performance year-in and year-out. Some periods will be better than others.

It seemed during the decade of the '80s, particularly the late '80s and into the early '90s, that large capitalization growth companies—which included a lot of technology companies—tended to have higher returns on equity and consequently higher stock prices—than any other group. After the three-year nuclear winter in corporate IT spending and no recovery in sight, valuations came down quite a bit.

Yet even during the decline, some of the dominant companies were still gaining market share in the markets they served. They didn't have much in the way of great earnings or revenue growth but balance sheet strengths grew, and they continued to maintain dominant market share

And that is something that should continue to happen in the future. Portfolios will be held to a higher standard of dependability in their financial performance.

We finally learned that technology bulldogs are cyclical, like anything else, which ultimately weakens their pedigree a bit.

So, in terms of expectations, the average growth stock might increase earnings anywhere from 6% to 7% over long periods of time. Those are the historic numbers. By definition, bulldogs are companies that have the potential to grow earnings from 10% to 15% a year annually over the long term.

As a result of this, chosen properly, and with a long enough time horizon, a Citizen Investor portfolio has the strong opportunity of providing above-average earnings growth and above-average total return.

To Every Season

Now in terms of how that above-average growth will appear, I would draw an analogy to a plant. Plants have seasons of growth, and then there are long periods where not much happens. You have to be around for the long term to appreciate the random nature and, over time, its immutable dependability.

It really is the same thing with stocks. In terms of earnings growth, generally, you'll want to find stocks that can produce over the longer term; that's what you are hoping for. You stick around and hopefully watch their earnings take off over time.

But again, it's rare to find a company that can grow at above-average rates for extended periods of time, and companies that can turn in 15% growth for 5, 10, 15 or 20 years are rarer still.

Still, that's what you are looking for, companies that have business models that allow them to deliver a superior track record.

Should you expect terrific growth in lousy markets, like the one we experienced at the start of this millennium?

I think there are cycles in almost every industry. What you want to be sure of is that the business model of the bulldog you have invested in is sound, and that the company maintains a dominant position in its industry, enabling you to predictably compare it against its competitors.

And if there is a downturn, you want to make sure they are indeed maintaining market share and their management's focus remains on opportunity. You want to see a continued commitment to research and development in order to maintain a sustainable competitive advantage.

If they do all that, odds are that they'll maintain that bulldog advantage.

But what if they don't?

How long do I give a failing bulldog before I shoot it?

It's when the business model changes. I have very rarely sold in advance of a negative surprise.

Having said that, I think our returns with bulldogs have been pretty reasonable over time. But if something changes, such as there is a big competitive threat or some condition in the marketplace—like higher costs, or scarcity of inventory—that really alters the business model, we would sell it.

And how long do you wait? I don't think it's a matter of time. I think it's basically when a bulldog no longer meets the 10-point checklist discussed previously, it's time for you to sell.

But you try to be rational about this and stay on a fairly even keel. And I think one of the keys to doing that is recognizing and understanding what you own. The companies in your portfolio have unique characteristics and financial guideposts. They have sales and earnings, and a balance sheet that you can read and become familiar with, and their performance over time will often reinforce certain expectations.

If the bulldog's managers do what they say they're going to do, if they go and deliver on what they promise, you are going to feel more confident. You believe they are going to hit their sales and earnings targets. That should help keep you on an even keel. It helps me.

The second thing that helps me—and indeed can help all of us—is the knowledge that if you are going to be a Citizen Investor, you have to learn to live with adversity. We saw earlier that the stock of Warren Buffett's Berkshire Hathaway fell 52% from peak to trough between 1998 and 2000.

Now this is a stock whose CEO is admittedly the best investor of his generation, possibly of all time. What his experience tells you is that as a condition of ownership, you have to learn to live with the vagaries of the market.

The history of investing is normally one where there are defeats as well as victories, but the long-term battle, as we have seen, is normally won by the person who owns companies today and holds on to them.

So, should you expect bulldogs will perform substantially better than other stocks? I think so.

I think two things account for that. First, the overall strategy that we have talked about throughout. You are trying to own somewhere between 13 and 20 good companies. With that many companies, providing you have them spread out across industries, you get about 90% of the benefits of total diversification you would get if you owned the market at large, and you get it without having to own the whole market.

My sense is that Philip Carret, the founder of Pioneer Funds, had it right when he said, "Never hold fewer than ten different securities covering five different fields of business."

My only caveat would be that you want to own real companies. You want to be buying robustly visible companies with solid balance sheets. In other words, these companies will not have a lot of debt and will be producing real earnings. I believe those kinds of firms will make up for the new potential Enrons and WorldComs that you also may buy along the way.

The second point is that as the market enters the 21st century a lot of people believe that small- and mid-caps will do much better than large-caps. Their thinking is that this recovery will mirror the recovery we saw after the vicious bear market of 1973–1974.

It probably will, and small cap mutual funds are a great way to participate in that, but I also believe dominant companies will benefit, as well.

It's my sense that scale has become very important in the world today, something that applies particularly to bulldogs. We're talking about formidable companies that tend to dominate their space. Through their business model, they exert extreme competitive advantage, either through big research and development budgets or because they have so much scale that they offer every product buyers might want and so, rather than go to multiple vendors, they go to this one bulldog and buy everything they need—including follow-up service.

Scale seems, to me, to be particularly important going forward in this world, and I think that benefit is going to accrue to Citizen Investors. That is where I am going to stick as the recovery unfolds.

I think right now, most folks are expecting earnings, as they have historically, to grow at maybe 7% a year for the S&P 500. I get interested in bulldogs when the earnings growth rate is above 10% and get really interested at 15%. If a company that I have found can grow 15% to 20% on a sustainable basis, that really gets me excited.

If we're right about these stocks and own them for long periods of time, I think it's realistic to expect a higher rate of return.

Why Settle for Average?

Average.

This is not the word you like to hear when your boss evaluates your performance at work or when friends describe your newborn son or daughter. When it comes to your investments, you definitely don't want the companies you invest in to be described this way or to be willing to settle for this in their own performance.

So, when you are thinking about the return on your money, average may be something you can reasonably expect, but I, for one, would hope you would aim higher.

I guess I am arguing the case for super bulldogs. I think that's basically what I'm trying to own: *the* dominant company, or companies, in major industries that can show some real growth. In the health area, for example, that would include pharmaceuticals, medical devices, biotechnology, diagnostics, and drug delivery.

But I'm trying to find the dominant ones. And so if you look for the dominant companies, you'll probably end up with a relatively short list. The question is which of the ones are going to excel, not which ones are going to survive.

My sense is that we may even see super bulldogs even more powerful than in the past possessing scale that will allow them to obtain that status.

Going forward, I'm looking for companies that exemplify traits of uncommon leadership. And if I had to pick two industries from which bulldogs would be likely to emerge from right now, one would be cable TV and the other would be medical devices.

Let's talk about cable first.

Cable companies currently, by and large, aren't profitable right now. They've spent, as a group, $50 billion over the last five years to enhance their networks to include high-speed Internet access which has beaten the heck out of DSL over phone lines, capturing share, and have basically won the war.

The second piece that makes them attractive is digital television.

As their capital expenditure budgets go down, as they are starting to right now, their margins will increase. Couple that with higher subscription rates—which are now $50 a month—and these companies become very appealing. If you throw Internet access on top of premium cable packages, you're seeing some of the providers getting as much as $150 a month on average for their services.

So this is an industry where cash flows presently look like they are going to go up dramatically over the long haul.

Cable has historically been a great business and has provided huge cash flows. And we're right at the watershed point, where the industry may be turning profitable. At this point, one would expect capital expenditures would go down dramatically and cash flows would go up. When that happens, you've potentially got a money machine.

The other area investors have been really excited about is medical devices. But, in addition, orthopedic companies are emerging as a good place to be, given the rapidly aging baby boomer generation. The number of hip and knee replacements that are done each year is high, and demand is going to remain strong for some time, as those baby boomers continue to age.

Part of the allure of these stocks is there is no competition from the drug industry. There's no drug that can compete with a knee replacement or a hip replacement, whereas a lot of internists still prescribe drugs even though implantable medical devices can often deliver better therapy. The same is holding true for many cardiac arrhythmia patients where devices are more effective than drugs.

So those are two areas where we think you're going to see important opportunities for promising performance.

Of all the thousands and thousands of publicly traded stocks, there are probably 100 to 150 that could legitimately be called bulldogs. The distinction? You want market leaders that are taking share and that have business models allowing them to thrive in good economies and bad.

My sense is that out of those 100 to 150 bulldogs, if you have a portfolio of 13 to 20, you're probably going to have three or four, maybe five that are just great stocks that you're probably never going to want to sell or, if you do sell, you'll only lighten up a little.

They should more than offset any problems that you have with the others, and that should make that 12% annualized return we have talked about very achievable.

R I S K

It's important to understand that as we transition from what noted investment author Nick Murray called a "nation of savers" to a "nation of investors," all of us will need to learn a different skill set: How to deal with risk. We have talked about the concept in passing, now we will focus on risk tolerance, the ability to coexist with ever-present risk that is critical to success as an investor

Let's start at the very beginning. Savers are risk averse. They're willing to lend you their assets if, in return over time, they are guaranteed a specific rate of return **and** their money back. Since there isn't much risk with this approach, there isn't much return.

In order to receive a greater return, you need to be willing to accommodate some risk, especially if you're seeking returns in the stock market.

Yes, there is market risk in the bond market. While you are holding on to your bond, its value will rise and fall inversely with interest rates. (When interest rates rise, the value of your bond will fall and vice versa.) But when your bond matures you can expect, except in the rarest of circumstances, to get your principal back.

With common stocks, you have market risk—will the stock market as a whole go up or down—as well as individual issue risk. Can the company you own go bankrupt? How will it perform in the stock market?

How you learn to live with risk is critically important.

Many people, maybe even you, were pretty much return-oriented during the big bull market years of the '90s. They bought whatever had worked without much examination of the risk involved. And being basically oblivious didn't hurt them because the "buy-the-dips" mentality worked, and the market just moved relentlessly higher no matter what you invested in.

But since the turn of the century, people certainly have learned the hard way that the market can go down and that there is serious risk involved in buying stocks.

The irony here is that if you look at the various asset classes, there's an important paradox. Those asset classes that are viewed as the least risky—i.e., CDs, money market funds, and Treasury bills—do not provide the compelling returns for the long term because of the impact of inflation and taxes on those assets. It is more than possible to lose ground by investing in cash equivalents for the long term. (See our earlier discussion on pages 126 & 127.)

What some people don't realize is that, based on historical data, stocks provide the greatest return. The investment that is the most risky in the short term—stocks—has proven over time to have been the most likely way to create wealth, as evidenced by the market's powerfully positive long-term compound return of better than 10% annually over decades of market history.

The take-away message: Stocks are the place to be if you are thinking long term, like planning for your retirement and post-retirement.

That post-retirement discussion is important. If a man retires at age 65, his life expectancy is in the 18-to-20-years range. For women, 20 years or more would not be uncommon. The specific number doesn't matter. The fact is that it's rare for an individual to have a large enough lump sum at age 65 to fund a retirement, particularly at the current 1.2 percent riskless T-bill rate.

So retirement time horizons are pretty long, and by definition if we're talking 15 to 20 years. That's certainly long enough to accommodate the risk that comes from holding equities as a portion of your retirement plan.

Most of us will be investors, pre-retirement and post-retirement, and a lot of people will own stocks well into their retirement years to provide adequate returns.

The secret here, when you are thinking about investing, is to let the timing of your goal determine your asset mix. If the goal is a year or two away, you don't want to be in stocks, and you may not even want to be in bonds. There is just too great a chance that you will lose principal before the time comes when you have to fund your goal.

But the longer the time period you have—5, 10, 15 years and beyond—then stocks are a pretty good answer. So to invest in stocks, you need to be where Peter Lynch and Warren Buffett have been—looking at three- to five-year time horizons at a minimum.

Let's go back to something we just touched on earlier. Assume your maximum time horizon is one year. Looking at the chart that follows, during the best one-year period you made 52% on your money. Conversely, during the worst year you lost 26%. What the chart depicts very graphically is that if your time horizon is only one year you're not investing, you're gambling. That's fine if entertainment's your goal, but I'd rather have a secure retirement.

Initial Value: $10,000 (12/31/72)		
	S&P 500 Index	
	Average Annual Total Returns	Portfolio Value
5 years later 12/31/72 – 12/31/77	-0.32%	$9,842
10 years later 12/31/72 – 12/31/82	6.63	19,010
15 years later 12/31/72 – 12/31/92	11.30	85,100
20 years later 12/31/72 – 12/31/97	13.04	214,133
Through 12/31/01	11.99	265,935

Source: Wiesneberger®.

Note: This performance is cited for illustrative purposes only. Past performance is no guarantee of future results, and this reference should not be construed as a recommendation to buy or sell any of the listed securities. Returns cited do not include fees or costs associated with the investment.

During the best five-year time frame, the highest return was 24%, the worst was –2.4%. The only five-year time period where you lost money ended Dec. 31, 1974; in all other five-year periods you made money. And when you look at the 10-year time frames, you always made money. Remember, we're talking about a raw index. Imagine how the odds go up if you're dealing with super quality growth or value companies.

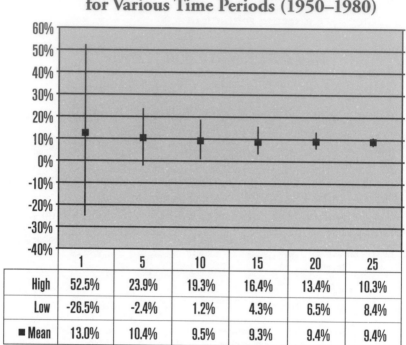

Range of Returns on Common Stocks for Various Time Periods (1950–1980)

	1	5	10	15	20	25
High	52.5%	23.9%	19.3%	16.4%	13.4%	10.3%
Low	-26.5%	-2.4%	1.2%	4.3%	6.5%	8.4%
■ Mean	13.0%	10.4%	9.5%	9.3%	9.4%	9.4%

Source: Vanguard Group
Does not reflect fees and costs
associated with the investment.

Year Periods

To quote respected investment writer Charles Ellis, "Time—the length of time investments will be held, the period of time over which investment results will be measured and judged—is the single most powerful factor in any investment program." While I can't improve on what Charles Ellis says, I can only state that you cannot truly understand and manage risk until you understand the importance of time.

BUT HOW DOES IT AFFECT ME?

You may now ask the question: "Suppose I can't sleep at night knowing that my stocks, even my bulldogs, may fall 50% in value. What do I do?"

If you suffer from that kind of fear—and if you do, you are not alone—the solution is simple. Only invest the portion of money where you could withstand a 50% loss. That's what asset allocation is all about.

Whenever I do speeches, people think my goal is to get them to put all their money in the stock market. Believe me, it isn't. It's to get them to recognize that once they have decided on a sum of money they choose to invest, it's best to leave it in the market, allowing the lever of time to do its work.

If you can't stand the volatility of the marketplace, invest a smaller amount of money. And recognize that the market is not for everyone. There are some people who just can't live with it.

There is nothing wrong with acknowledging that, but you also need to recognize that an extremely conservative portfolio probably won't allow you to achieve your goals.

For example, it is going to be very difficult for people to reach retirement goals using just cash and bonds. The risks are a little different with each, but the results are the same, as we touched on before.

With cash, if you look at the returns for T-bills, a proxy for cash, going back to 1926, you'll see that the annualized return is about 3.8% a year. As we said previously, inflation has averaged 3.1% over that time, so that leaves you 0.7% as a return and that is before you pay taxes. It's a pretty measly reward on your investment, and as we have seen the return could actually be negative, depending on your tax rate.

Bonds fared a little better. The long-term government bond delivered a 5.3% return on average, going back to 1926, so once you took inflation into account, you ended up with a 2.2% return, but again, that was before you paid taxes on it. Corporate bonds returned 5.7%. You can do the math.

And then remember, with bonds you have both investment risk—the risk that the value of your bond could fall as interest rates rise—and reinvestment risk. When your bonds mature, will interest rates be at or above where they were when you bought the bond in the first place? If they are, the yield you will get when you reinvest your bonds' proceeds in additional bonds will be less.

Again, you want to go with the asset mix you are comfortable with, but you have to remember that being too risk-averse can erode long-term return potential.

THE OTHER KIND OF RISK

It's also important to recognize that with individual issues, there's a risk aside from market risk. A stock can go down in a down market, but the true risk for me in investing in bulldogs is that I'm wrong on my assumption of the company's ability to consistently deliver superior financial performance. That's execution risk, and it's the prime risk for me in investing in bulldogs.

Here's an example of a company that, unfortunately, lost its bulldog status as described by financial columnist Scott Burns in the *Dallas Morning News*. In 1981, if you were talking about the future of technology, you had to mention Digital Equipment Corporation (DEC). The Massachusetts firm, founded by some brilliant men from MIT, appeared by most accounts to be on track to become one of the first of the technology bulldogs. As the industry leader in the fledgling computer business, the firm was ranked by *Forbes* that year as the 37th most valuable firm in America, ahead of Coca-Cola, Intel, Motorola and Texas Instruments. The ranking was largely based on its powerful (for the time) mini-computers that were used by companies to power dumb terminals throughout an organization. While IBM and Apple were creating personal computers, DEC CEO Ken Olsen believed in these small mainframe computers as the future of technology in America. PCs, he believed, were for hobbyists.

Summary Statistics of Annual Total Returns (1926–2002)

Series	Mean	Distribution
Large Company Stocks	10.2%	
Small Company Stocks	12.1	
Long-Term Corporate Bonds	5.9	
Long-Term Government	5.9	
Intermediate-Term Government	5.4	
U.S. Treasury Bills	3.8	
Inflation	3.0	

*The 1933 Small Company Stocks Total Return was 142.9 percent.
Source: Ibbotson Associates

-90%   0%   90%

Fast-forward 16 years and the same list ranked DEC as the 337th most valuable firm. What happened to DEC? The market for its products changed, and the company didn't. DEC tried to get in on the personal computing trend, but its WP78 was a $4,995 machine that was used mostly for word processing. The firm, along with Cray, Control Data, and a few others, made its bet on mainframe computing. The market still exists and is a valuable one, but it has long been eclipsed by the remarkably powerful PCs that are used by nearly every American.

In the end, DEC was bought by Compaq, which itself was acquired by Hewlett-Packard. The moral here is that individual issues have a risk above and beyond the market risk. This individual issue risk can be offset somewhat by using diversified portfolios. If you have a Citizen Investor portfolio of bulldogs, you want to own at least 13 of them, spread over four or five industries.

If I don't understand the difference between individual risk and market risk, I may dump good stocks. I may look at my bulldog that is getting hammered along with the rest of the market and think I better sell because it's going to go lower, when the reality is that there is absolutely nothing wrong with the stocks, other than this is a time when people are fleeing all equities.

Basically, any company could come upon a spell of selling. It's not uncommon with the natural rotation in the marketplace for industry groups to be dragged down from time to time.

For example, during the Internet bubble, so-called "old economy" stocks fell completely out of favor. While high-flying Internet infrastructure and other technology stocks took center stage, no one wanted to hear about old-fashioned bricks-and-mortar retailers. Those stocks traded down and created a huge buying opportunity basically because the market eventually reverted to what it's always done and awarded those stocks with higher prices.

So the market volatility from time to time can take down good stocks along with the bad and give people buying opportunities. You're probably going to be a more astute investor if you're paying attention to the financials and understand that during a decline, the company's business franchise is still powerful and strong and that once a recovery comes, it will revert to the old ability to deliver above-average earnings growth.

If you are just looking at the volatility alone, your confidence can be shaken and it can lead you to sell a desirable company just because of the way the overall market is reacting.

Stock market returns have been around 10% a year on average, versus 3% for cash and 5% for bonds. The irony here is that over long periods, the investment people consider the most risky—stocks—have historically been the most likely way to create and protect wealth against the ravages of inflation.

DON'T THINK, CONCENTRATE

Now, let's take what we have talked about so far a step further.

If you are investing in stocks, the more stocks from diverse industries you own, the more diversified you are. That's both good and (sort of) bad.

It's "good" in the sense that if one stock tanks, you are not hurt too badly. But it's "bad" because the more stocks you own, the more likely it is by definition that you will get an average equity return because stellar performance of superior companies is reduced back to the mean as you increase the number of stocks you own. You can't outperform the market if you own the market.

Of course, owning a mutual fund is a very different approach to investing in the market. You spread your risk across a much larger universe of companies. This ensures that your holdings are not seriously hurt by the downturn of an individual firm, but it also limits the upside of a market winner.

The advantage of the Citizen Investor approach is that you gain more upside but, as a *Journal of Finance* study of risk spread over 15 to 20 stocks showed, you also can get almost all the benefits of market diversification even though you have a much smaller holding of large capitalization stocks. Every investment has risk, of course, and the Citizen Investor approach is not immune.

Remember that the Citizen Investor portfolio makes sense only as it represents a portion of your equity holdings. Because you will likely use widely diversified alternatives, it makes some sense to consider the importance of concentrating what you own. Basically, you can buy a fund of great large-cap companies, really visible, great franchises and own an interest in 60 to 200 companies. Or, as we have said throughout, you can buy 13 bulldogs and get 90% of the benefits of diversification but infinitely better upside in my opinion.

The reason this approach can work is twofold:

1. You have other equity holdings to offset some of the risk of concentrating here, and

2. There are above-average companies out there that have the ability to deliver superior earnings growth. My hope is that I can get a return that's above that of the market's 10% with this portion of my portfolio.

In summary, the overriding risk of a bulldog portfolio is that the company's business model deteriorates, not that its stock price falls.

GOING FORWARD

We talked about having a sufficient amount of your money in stocks, both to get the growth you need, and to offset what inflation can do to your investments. Despite what has happened in 2000–2002, I think 10 years from now the percentage of people who have money in equities will be higher than it is today. People will have gotten more accustomed to investing their money in retirement plans. They'll be more confident.

Right now, I think people are challenged by that. We have come off a couple of bad years in the market, and people still don't feel good about owning stocks, and they aren't willing to buy or make a commitment to equities.

This gets us back to the importance of feeling confident. Everyone has to answer for himself or herself how much they should have invested in stock. The higher the percentage of stocks in your retirement plan, for example, the more money you should have when it comes time to retire, if history repeats itself, as I believe it will.

The higher the percentage, the greater the likelihood over time you will have a better return on your money, but it is up to you to decide how much risk you are willing to assume.

Now, in determining that, I think you've got to look ahead. Right now, after a three-plus year bear market where

The Power of Time (1926–2001)

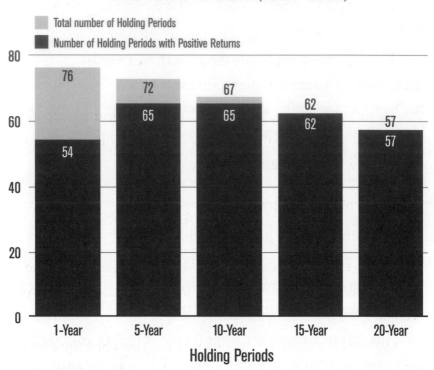

Total number of Holding Periods
Number of Holding Periods with Positive Returns

Holding Periods

Source: Ibbotson Associates, Chicago. Stocks are represented by the Standard & Poor's 500 Index.

we've had terrible erosion to assets, the last thing most people are willing to do is pour everything they own into the market. At the moment, most people are in a state of denial about the damage to their portfolios and consequently have a very low tolerance for risk.

But, as the chart illustrates, it's important to recognize the historical perspective, because it's a great teacher. Owning stocks is a lot like having kids. You worry about them. There's no way to feel great all the time if you are an investor. There's no way to be an owner of stocks and make money every single day. It can't be done.

There is going to be risk. And you have to grow accustomed to that. It's an important step.

I think a thorough understanding of risk and reward is really critical to investing, and you should only invest up to the point where you can sleep at night.

Final Thoughts About Risk

I hope this book, coupled with the opportunity that the democratization of capitalism provides, stimulates people to recognize the importance of ownership.

I've talked a lot about investment concepts but the one thing that keeps coming back to me when I do speeches or talk to clients is that they understand the whole concept of bulldog almost intuitively.

Once an investor has that confidence, they go out and search for other bulldogs, find them, buy them, and keep them. There just aren't that many good ones, and once you own a good one, you ought to keep it. As we have talked about throughout, the real risk of owning a bulldog comes from selling it too soon.

CONCLUSION

In the first chapter, I talked about how my brother and I created an investment account that allowed my mother to have a successful retirement. It was an experience that opened my eyes to how powerful the combination of time and investing in dominant companies can be. Today, stepping back from the day-to-day ups and downs of the market and looking at the last twenty-eight years since we did that, I'm stunned by how obvious it is that this approach can work. While the companies my brother and I put my mother's money into would not all be the same ones we would recommend today, the theme of market dominance, of finding bulldogs, remains the same.

CONCLUSION

I know it can be hard to believe in the face of the past two-plus years of overwhelmingly bad news, of corporate executives being led away in handcuffs, of dot.com catastrophes, and real catastrophes caused by terrorists in our own country and war in the Middle East. I'm asked all the time about these issues and whether they will take the market so far off course that it won't recover.

For the answer, I look to history. Through two world wars, a host of recessions, the Depression of my parents' youth, banking scandals, and two stock market crashes, the market has recovered and continued its march ever higher, in defiance of the nay-sayers. The market's record represents the growth that can naturally occur when democracy and capitalism co-exist. Just as we didn't fold in the face of Y2K, Americans have proven an historic ability to pull together and succeed in the face of even the most overwhelming odds. A bet against us has always proven to be the wrong one. I am convinced that remains true, when it comes to the stock market or anything else.

In this book, I hope I've given you a fresh look at managing risk and reward, and offered you a new way of viewing the market. Now that we're almost done, let's isolate the fine points.

Let's Review

The following are the answers to the most frequently asked questions I get when I do seminars or speeches. This will serve as a good device for retaining what we have learned. (And if you are one of those people who read the conclusion first, it will serve as a good introduction to where we are heading.)

What is the most important take-away message from *The Citizen Investor*?

Just like the old parable, it involves teaching people how to fish rather than just giving them a fish.

If you give people a stock, you have given them one idea that might work for a day. But if you teach them to find valuable stocks, you have given them ideas for a lifetime. And I hope that's what we have done here. Instead of just giving you a list of stocks to buy, we've tried to teach you a formula for producing solid investment returns.

To me, what this book is about is building and gaining the confidence one derives from being a patient owner of great businesses. Once you've gained this confidence, you can tolerate risk effectively and build wealth.

Are there other important messages?

Let me give you three.

1. The first take-away point is to own businesses. Don't trade stock certificates; i.e., don't move in and out of specific stocks. Keep score by focusing on the company's financial performance and not the daily ups and downs of its share price.

Don't trade certificates based on price fluctuations. Price, over time, always follows financial performance.

If I could choose one desirable criterion for a stock, it would be stable, above-average earnings growth.

Ultimately, earnings will win out as the most powerful long-term catalyst for stock valuation.

2. The second theme to stress is the importance of thinking long term. Long term isn't just a hiding place for strategists like me to admit that we don't know what's going on in the short term. Longer time periods, say three to five years, allow time for the market to interpret, weigh and price your company's financial performance. Longer time periods not only lower the impact of market volatility, but provide you with a lower tax rate (i.e., long-term capital gains vs. ordinary income) when you sell a holding.

I would argue that the two best investors we have seen in our collective lifetimes have been Peter Lynch and Warren Buffett. The returns on the funds they managed have been nothing short of astonishing. I don't think it is a coincidence that both men are long-term investors.

Think three- to five-year time horizons at a minimum.

3. The final take-away is to remember how rare great companies are. Great companies that can deliver above-average earnings growth year after year after year are extraordinarily few and far between. Once you find one, you ought to hold on to it.

What should I conclude from your first two answers?

Virtually all great investors were or are long-term investors. They don't try to buy a stock so they can trade it the next day. They don't buy tips. They don't buy initial public offerings.

Warren Buffett defined his style of investing as kind of like watching paint dry. He said, "I'm amazed when a stock I buy goes up in the short term."

Second, the longer your time horizon, the more likely it is you will make money. That is what history has proven in the stock market.

Third, in my opinion, we now are at an attractive point in our nation's history to receive solid investment returns. We're at the cusp of a trend of ownership I believe will reward fortunate ones, the ones who will invest like savvy business owners. Capitalism, combined with democracy, isn't perfect, but as the last 20 years show, it has no serious rivals and works more effectively than any other economic and political system out there.

The point here is that you now have a chance to own shares of great businesses and treat that position as if you own the whole company. We were at one time a nation of farmers. Now, we're presented with the opportunity to own a stake in America's future. That beats betting on the price direction of a rented certificate.

I've written this book to amplify the opportunity people can choose to take if they want to add long-term ownership to their portfolio or augment their managed solutions like mutual funds. My suggestion has been to focus on the raw ownership of great businesses. And I would submit that it's not all that difficult to find a list of great ones. Maybe you need some professional help in terms of structuring portfolios and in terms of what to look for, but my sense is that the democratization of capitalism is a great event and it's a trend, I think, that's going to help a lot of people meet their retirement goals by learning that acting like owners helps them to manage risk.

But the question is how are you going to find these great businesses? From the media? I don't think that is the way to go. The media's what's-on-the-table-TODAY attitude tends to override the anticipatory instincts essential to good investment thinking. For most of the media—be it television or print—their job is to entertain. So given that, always remember they are more likely to focus on the successes and failures of the recent past and not on forward-looking investment information.

Remember, investing is about anticipating what could happen, not reacting to what has happened. I am in the investment business, not the entertainment business. It's not my goal to entertain you, although I hope you haven't found what I have had to say dull. It's my goal to try to help you manage risk and reap rewards over time.

That's why I've talked so much about ownership. Look around at your local community; look at the people who are wealthy. They're wealthy because they own something—the local car dealership, the grocery, their own business. And what's exciting to me about the democratization of capitalism is that it gives you a chance to participate as an owner/investor of great companies.

Owning individual companies is a full-contact endeavor, not a spectator sport. Becoming engaged with solid risk management tools and superior companies is a recipe for success that I believe will lead to enhanced popularity of individual stock ownership.

What I am talking about here is an activity where you become engaged and thereby gain that confidence I spoke about earlier, the confidence that comes from being an owner. When I do a seminar with people and we discover we share a common thread—we both own Medtronic or Pfizer or a company that's really delivered over the last 5, 10, 15 years— we know that although the market price may decline, as a leader, the core business is still strong and it is very likely to evolve and emerge a stronger company. So, we don't sell. We own.

We have confidence. And I think that is important because it goes to the heart of the question every investor asks when they hear anyone giving advice. That question is: "Why should I care?" And the most basic answer there is another question: If you're calling the shots in your retirement plan, isn't a position of confidence a good place to be?

I think we tend to be better at things we understand. Investing is not rocket science. Owning good businesses is not the exclusive activity of Mensa members. If you feel inadequate when it comes to determining when to buy and sell, and you need one excellent investment tool to rely on, read the annual report. Focus on what the chairperson and/or president say his or her goals are for earnings and revenue growth. And then own the companies that do what they say they're going to do. And those that don't, sell them.

The final reason is the most powerful one. Investing in a Citizen Investor portfolio of bulldogs probably has the same risk as investing overall, but I think it gives the opportunity for higher returns. While I can't promise you'll beat the market, I sincerely believe you'll receive returns that compensate for the risk taken.

What should the equity portion of my portfolio look like? Where do the bulldogs fit in?

I think you need to do an asset allocation plan with a financial professional to figure out what your split of stocks, bonds, and cash should look like. A very important investment decision is how you divide up your assets.

As you determine your asset allocation, I would recommend that you keep in mind that you may be retired for up to 30 years, and that means you are probably always going to be a stock investor of some sort. For most of us, loading up your portfolio exclusively with bonds and cash simply won't allow you a return that fulfills your retirement goals.

Ideally, the stock portion of your retirement plan will always include both growth and value styles of investing, along with the broad exposure utilizing all capitalization levels.

Here's a sample portfolio:

60–65% large-cap;

20% mid-cap;

15–20% small-cap

The growth style of investing has been out of favor now for almost three years. It may make sense for some investors to consider a contrarian posture and favor a heavier weighting to the growth style.

Per my prescription, as much as 45% of total equity could be committed to large-cap growth investing. You could use a mutual fund to fulfill your needs, but that isn't what this book is about. I believe you can use a portfolio of carefully selected bulldogs to meet your large-cap growth needs. This is the part of my personal equity portfolio in which I have my greatest confidence. Done properly, it will give you the same feeling.

What does the bulldog portion of my portfolio look like?

I would recommend that people invest in at least four or five industries, or themes, they think are promising.

Here are some examples:

◆ **Health care,** I suspect, is going to be a powerful beneficiary of the graying of America.

◆ **Technology** has a self-fulfilling future based on the huge leaps of productivity we enjoy (once businesses decide to begin spending again).

◆ New value propositions for the consumer via innovations in **retailing.**

◆ The inexorable elimination of middlemen in delivering **financial services** is another opportunity-rich investment theme.

(A *Journal of Finance* study in 1968 showed that you can obtain market-like investment diversification by holding as few as 10 large capitalization stocks. The study indicated that you accomplish virtually all of the diversification of the market by holding 14 individual stocks, and adding a 15th does not appreciably enhance diversification.)

This type of portfolio concentration provides the potential of higher-than-market returns with market-like risk characteristics.

As I look at a lot of client portfolios, they don't have 13 stocks; they either have too few or they have too many. My sense is that with a large-capitalization, dominant-company strategy if you have four or five industries covered with 13 to

20 stocks, that's adequate. Equally dollar-weight each of the companies.

A minimum would be 13 stocks, equally weighted, spread across four or five industries or themes. Industry allocations could mirror S&P weightings. If the S&P currently has 21 percent weighting in financials, you could commit 21 percent of your assets to financials and weight equally with two or three stocks.

How hard is it to implement this strategy?

For simplicity's sake you could just buy an equal dollar amount of the 13 or whatever the number of the bulldogs you want to invest in.

Then you want to gauge each quarter as it comes in. Are the companies meeting the goals they set? Is this company's management doing what they say they're going to do? And if they do tend to deliver over time, you keep them. If not, you sell.

There are going to be business models that fail, and that is the risk in this approach. When we talk about risk, in Citizen Investor, we have redefined it. We aren't focusing on market risk. Rather, we are talking about how effectively a company executes all the things that management said it was going to do. Were they correct in their assessment of the company's future, and can they meet it? That's the risk here. Does the business model fail or not do as well as management said it would?

Owners focus on the financial health of their enterprise, not its market price.

Do I rebalance my portfolio periodically?

There's always the argument about rebalancing when you have a big winner, especially as it grows to become a bigger and bigger part of your portfolio. Should you sell some and use the proceeds to rebalance your portfolio?

Ideally, what we have talked about is a low-turnover kind of strategy. You only sell when you're wrong, and out of the 13 to 20 stocks you own, you may find that you may be wrong about two or three times a year. Or you might not be wrong, but you could find something that will form the basis for you selling. For example, the company is acquiring a new, higher-risk business or has entered into a joint venture that negatively alters the business dynamic that made you a buyer in the first place.

A stock falling in price is the worst reason to sell a company you believe is a bulldog. All stocks experience periods of price decline. It's natural. As long as you believe in a company's fundamentals, you should stick with it. Remember Peter Lynch's comment about selling too soon.

Rebalancing, though, is somewhat different than selling. My sense is that you may want to lighten up if one or two of your bulldogs become substantial winners, although I'm reminded of Warren Buffett who doesn't tend to rebalance. Historically, he has owned the same companies for long periods of time, and he has done incredibly well.

The one advantage to rebalancing is you tend to take advantage of high prices to sell a portion of your position. And lowering the risk in your portfolio is always a good idea. Still, you need to consider the tax impact of rebalancing. You may find yourself with capital gains that will impact your returns.

Rebalancing is a personal choice. You should go through the exercise once a year, maybe at a regular interval, like on your birthday. Based on the performance of each stock, you can decide whether or not to rebalance. It's really up to you.

However, I'm not in favor of doubling down. If you own a stock where the market says you're wrong, and you are convinced you're not, instead of investing more money into it, you're probably wiser to go buy another stock rather than pour more money into it. That way you hedge your bets a bit.

Can I implement this bulldog strategy on my own?

Yes, it's possible.

That said, I think having a broker or some other financial professional you can rely on is very important. This person can tailor the information flow for you and provide a professional level of guidance that includes answering questions as well as providing inevitable reality checks every investor needs.

A lot of people think the final goal is to pick up your monthly statement and be rewarded from the one-time decisions you have made. I find that doesn't happen often. One needs to be a little more active and understand the dynamics of the companies within the portfolio.

You can do this on your own, but having a knowledgeable financial professional as a trusted advocate of your best financial interest is well worth its cost. Remember the old legal saw: "The lawyer who represents himself has a fool for a client."

Why doesn't everybody do this?

Probably they don't know about it, although unconsciously, I think many investors have a favorite stock. You can see that in the fact that they end up buying a local bulldog. In Minneapolis, it's Medtronic. In Seattle, it's Microsoft. Other parts of the country have their own great stocks. And those are the ones that everybody nods their heads in understanding. They hold them up as exemplary companies and want to own as many shares as they can.

But my point is you should consider building a portfolio of great businesses, instead of just buying one or two. We at RBC Dain Rauscher, and other professionals, can help you work up a screen of great companies and then determine which are the best for creating wealth in your retirement plan.

If you watch the media—both print and TV—the focus is on what is working now. This is not the critical focus essential to preparing for financial outcomes years from now. Today, *Barron's* and *The Wall Street Journal* are actually recommending hundreds of stocks. I believe this also fosters the illusion that activity is good. We absolutely can't help but feel we are missing the boat if our focus isn't on today's or this week's outcome. Serious outcomes are planned years in advance.

Another reason everybody doesn't do it is they don't understand that there are so few great companies. It's not necessarily their fault. I mean, if you look at CNBC, CNNfn and Bloomberg, the people on the air focus on a small number of news-making companies. What makes news is generally not positive. The really successful companies may slip under the radar.

You hope that they'll be there to tell you when the wheels are going to come off or be there to warn you when conditions change for the company. But my sense is that not a lot of people understand how rare these good companies are and what an advantage it is just to buy and hold them, not trying to trade them.

What could distract people from following this approach?

The main reason is that there are inevitable periods of decline. It's the same thing that's keeping people from buying Dogs of the Dow, which is a contrarian strategy, where you buy the least favorite stocks in the Dow. The Dogs of the Dow strategy forces you to buy large-cap companies that normally don't go out of business, companies that have relatively high yields, at times when they're unpopular and hoping they will bounce back over time.

The Dogs of the Dow system has worked historically. The reason people using this approach fail, is because if it doesn't work for a certain period, they think it won't ever be succesful again and so they go on to the next strategy that might work. Some misinformed souls travel from idea to idea, never sticking with the one or two disciplines and letting anticipation and time do their work for them.

And as a broker, the job I had when I first got into this business, I can tell you that chasing the hot trend is a loser's game. Look at the great money managers. They don't change their style. They find an approach that they're confident in and they stick with it, recognizing that there will be periods when their style doesn't work. As we've seen, there have been periods when even Warren Buffett has had down years. But in the face of declines that dropped the value of his holding more than 50% he stuck with his strategy, understanding that even he wasn't nimble enough to sell everything ahead of market declines and get back in as the stock market took his stocks higher.

You have to live with the volatility of the market in order to extract the superior long-term premium returns.

So why doesn't everybody do it? It's the adversity of the market that could take them out of the game. Remember, you're not a saver. You're an investor. With regard to our stock portfolio, we need to be more risk-tolerant, not risk-averse.

What are the evil consequences if I don't follow your advice?

I'm reminded of presidential economic advisor Bernard Baruch's comments. He said: "There are no bears living on Park Avenue."

To me, the only evil consequence is that you miss out on a wonderful opportunity. This is a reasonably simple system to follow and execute.

However, it does require some things that do not resonate in a skeptic's lexicon—conviction. It's always worked in the past. Superior companies that deliver above-average earnings growth over time do reward their investors. But I think anybody who's a skeptic or a pessimist is going to have a really difficult time with this. Basically, this is not a program for skeptics but for optimists who recognize that there are wonderful companies out there that can generate handsome returns to patient investors.

What's the proof that your approach works?

The best example of the last 30 years is the Morgan Guaranty Nifty Fifty, the list of big-cap stocks that led the bull market of the late '60s that subsequently cratered in the downturn of the early '70s. The conventional wisdom has been that this was a disaster for investors.

But, if you take a look at the list of stocks, you see many of them have survived to become household names; some of them could be considered bulldogs. After all, the list includes IBM, Texas Instruments Merck, Pfizer, Eli Lilly, American Home Products, Sears, J.C. Penney, Avon, McDonald's, and Kodak.

And, when you look at the performance of the group, you see the power of time, even with stocks that went through a serious decline in value.

For example, if you bought them in December of 1972, at the peak of their value, you would have lost 80% of your money during the decline of 1973. But if you held on, by 1980 you would have broken even and by 1999, as we have seen, you would have done almost as well as the S&P 500. When people talk about declining stocks and the lessons of history, they would do well to look at this example.

Meanwhile, there are bulldogs being created as we speak. To understand how that happens, let's look back at our original examples of Circuit City and Best Buy, the stars of the '80s and '90s.

Think back to the late '70s and early '80s when the most high-tech piece of equipment in most homes was the self-cleaning oven. An Apple II computer was an unimaginable device that seemed to serve no practical purpose when you could play Pong on your television. When you bought your TV or hi-fi, you probably turned to Sears, Montgomery Wards, or a local TV shop that spent as much time repairing as it did selling electronics.

That all changed by the mid-'80s with the introduction of the compact disc and video cassette recorder, two of the most quickly accepted pieces of consumer technology in history. By the '90s—you know the rest of the story. The consumer electronics market became crowded with devices for every part of our lives, from PDAs, PCs and cell phones, to DVDs and camcorders. Circuit City in the '80s and Best Buy in the '90s were able to take advantage of the creation of this market. Anyone who invested in them from the start was richly rewarded.

Somewhere, in some developing market we may not even be aware of, the bulldogs of the new millennium are being created.

As I sum up my thoughts, I would like to leave you with these three lessons as they apply to Citizen Investors:

1. The Citizen Investor approach provides you with the opportunity to develop an uncommon confidence that can only come from owning superior businesses. This feeling has traditionally been reserved for the wealthy, who were the only ones who could afford to own businesses, leaving the door shut for the rest of us. Now, you may choose to join them by owning shares of great companies. Once you do, you'll gain a feeling you can't get from trading certificates or trying to time a market that seems, at times, to react more and more irrationally. You'll know what I'm talking about when you see your bulldogs prosper, while others struggle through euphoric highs and desolate lows.

2. The secret of success in the long term is that there is no secret. This isn't rocket science, and there are no shortcuts. The stock market has a very effective way of weeding out all but the best firms and rewarding the ownership approach. By becoming a patient owner of superior businesses, you will be rewarded.

3. There are NOT that many great companies to own. When you find one and the company continues to deliver superior operating results, you ought to hold on to it.

ONE LAST THOUGHT

If you find yourself watching business television and sweating each point of a stock on the way up and on the way down, you are a trader, you have entered the stock market casino and, considering transaction costs and taxes, the odds are not in your favor.

When the trading approach works, it's a giddy way to make money. But when it doesn't, and that's more often than not, it's a depressing ride down.

We in the investment business know this all too well. We've lived it for at least two-and-a-half years. It's up to each of us to step away from the card table and begin to get serious about growing the resources we will need for the rest of our lives.

I challenge you to take that step, knowing that investing always has risks, but also knowing there are companies that will stand the test of time. When you own them, you become the ideal that is the Citizen Investor.

Take that step.

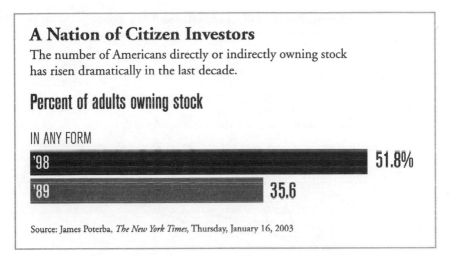

A Nation of Citizen Investors

The number of Americans directly or indirectly owning stock
has risen dramatically in the last decade.

Percent of adults owning stock

IN ANY FORM

'98   **51.8%**

'89   **35.6**

Source: James Poterba, *The New York Times*, Thursday, January 16, 2003

A History of Inflation-Beating Returns

The Value of $1,000 Invested from 1926–2002

Source: Ibbotson Associates, Chicago.

Note: This performance is cited for illustrative purposes only. Past performance is no guarantee of future results, and this reference
should not be construed as a recommendation to buy or sell any of the listed securities. Returns cited do not include fees or costs
associated with the investment.

Stocks, Bonds, Bills, and Inflation 1925–2002
Wealth indices of investments in the U.S. capital markets*

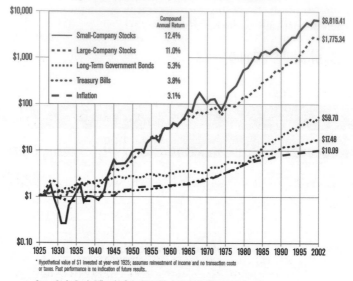

* Hypothetical value of $1 invested at year-end 1925; assumes reinvestment of income and no transaction costs
or taxes. Past performance is no indication of future results.

Source: Stocks, Bonds, Bills and Inflation® 2003 Yearbook, ©2001 Ibbotson Associates, Inc.
Based on copyrighted works by Ibbotson and Sinquefield. All rights reserved. Used with permission.

Dollar Cost Averaging: By the Numbers			
Month	Regular Investment	Share Price	Shares Acquired
January	$300	$10	30
February	$300	$5	60
March	$300	$10	30
April	$300	$25	12
May	$300	$15	20
Total	$1,500	*	152

*The average share price over that time was $13. Yet, by using dollar averaging, you would have paid $9.87 for your shares. The numbers above reflect a hypothetical scenario and are for illustrative purposes only.

Trying to Time the Market Can Be Costly
December 31, 1991–December 31, 2002

Period of Investment	Average Annual Total Return	Growth of $10,000
Fully Invested	10.65%	$27,526
Missed the 10 Best Days	5.99%	$17,887
Missed the 20 Best Days	2.63%	$12,968
Missed the 30 Best Days	-0.08%	$9,920
Missed the 40 Best Days	-2.48%	$7,782

Source: Bloomberg. The stock market is represented by the Standard & Poor's 500 Index.

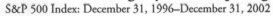

In-and-Out Investors:
Penalized for Missing Key Market Upswings
S&P 500 Index: December 31, 1996–December 31, 2002

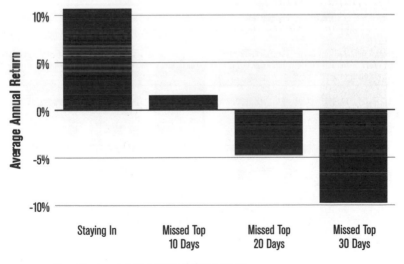

Source: Bloomberg calculations by Van Kampen Investments, Inc.

Rolling-Period Returns
S&P 500 Index: December 31, 1950–December 31, 2002

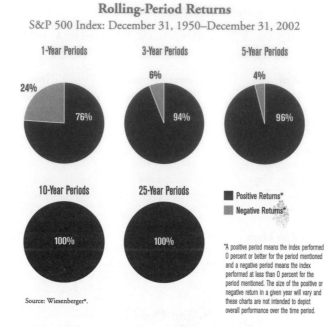

1-Year Periods

24%

76%

3-Year Periods

6%

94%

5-Year Periods

4%

96%

10-Year Periods

100%

25-Year Periods

100%

■ Positive Returns*

■ Negative Returns*

*A positive period means the index performed 0 percent or better for the period mentioned and a negative period means the index performed at less than 0 percent for the period mentioned. The size of the positive or negative return in a given year will vary and these charts are not intended to depict overall performance over the time period.

Source: Wiesenberger*.

The Power of Time (1926–2001)

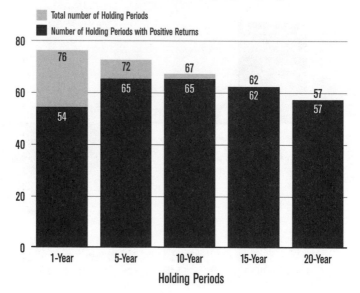

■ Total number of Holding Periods
■ Number of Holding Periods with Positive Returns

80

76

72

67

62

57

65

65

62

57

60

54

40

20

0

1-Year   5-Year   10-Year   15-Year   20-Year

Holding Periods

Source: Ibbotson Associates, Chicago. Stocks are represented by the Standard & Poor's 500 Index.

Summary Statistics of Annual Total Returns (1926–2002)

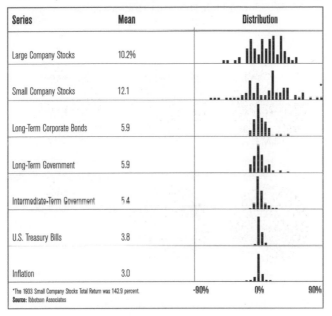

Series	Mean	Distribution
Large Company Stocks	10.2%	
Small Company Stocks	12.1	
Long-Term Corporate Bonds	5.9	
Long-Term Government	5.9	
Intermediate-Term Government	5.4	
U.S. Treasury Bills	3.8	
Inflation	3.0	

*The 1933 Small Company Stocks Total Return was 142.9 percent.
Source: Ibbotson Associates

-90%   0%   90%

Range of Returns on Common Stocks for Various Time Periods (1950–1980)

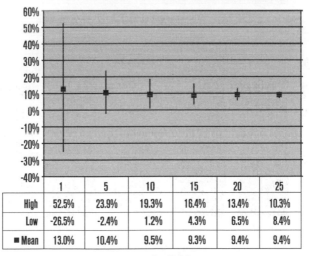

	1	5	10	15	20	25
High	52.5%	23.9%	19.3%	16.4%	13.4%	10.3%
Low	-26.5%	-2.4%	1.2%	4.3%	6.5%	8.4%
■ Mean	13.0%	10.4%	9.5%	9.3%	9.4%	9.4%

Year Periods

Source: Vanguard Group
Does not reflect fees and costs
associated with the investment.

A Little Difference Can Mean a Lot						
$10,000 invested for this many years	4% annual return	6% annual return	8% annual return	10% annual return	12% annual return	14% annual return
1	10,400	10,600	10,800	11,000	11,200	11,400
5	12,166	13,382	14,693	16,105	17,623	19,254
10	14,802	17,908	21,589	25,932	31,058	37,072
15	18,009	23,965	31,721	41,772	54,735	71,379
20	21,911	32,072	46,609	67,275	96,462	137,434
25	26,658	42,918	68,484	108,347	170,000	264,619
30	32,433	57,434	100,626	174,454	299,599	509,501

*This chart presents a hypothetical scenario for illustrative purposes only. Returns depicted do not take into account fees, commissions, or other expenses associated with investments.

Initial Value: $10,000 (12/31/72)

	S&P 500 Index	
	Average Annual Total Returns	Portfolio Value
5 years later 12/31/72 – 12/31/77	-0.32%	$9,842
10 years later 12/31/72 – 12/31/82	6.63	19,010
15 years later 12/31/72 – 12/31/92	11.30	85,100
20 years later 12/31/72 – 12/31/97	13.04	214,133
Through 12/31/01	11.99	265,935

Source: Wiesneberger®.

Note: This performance is cited for illustrative purposes only. Past performance is no guarantee of future results, and this reference should not be construed as a recommendation to buy or sell any of the listed securities. Returns cited do not include fees or costs associated with the investment.